EARLY
AMERICAN DRAMATISTS

From the Beginnings to 1900

WORLD DRAMATISTS

In the same series:

WORLD DRAMATISTS

ARLY

AMERICAN

DRAMATISTS

From the Beginnings to 1900

JACK A. VAUGHN

WITH PHOTOGRAPHS

FREDERICK UNGAR PUBLISHING CO.

NEW YORK

Copyright © 1981
by Frederick Ungar Publishing Co., Inc.
Printed in the United States of America
Design by Edith Fowler

Library of Congress Cataloging in Publication Data

Vaughn, Jack A   1935–
  Early American dramatists.

  (World dramatists)
  Bibliography: p.
  Includes index.
  1. American drama—History and criticism.
2. Theater—United States—History. I. Title.
PS341.V39   812'.009   80-53703
ISBN 0-8044-2940-5

CONTENTS

CHRONOLOGY

1665   *Ye Bare and Ye Cubb* is performed in August in Virginia. Although the text of the play has not survived, this is the earliest record of English-language theatrical activity on the North American continent.

1700   The Assembly of Pennsylvania issues a ban on "stage plays, masks, revels" and other "rude and riotous sports," thus initiating a succession of such legislative prohibitions in most of the Colonies.

1702   A "pastoral colloquy" is performed at the College of William and Mary. This is the earliest record of academic drama in America.

1703   Anthony Aston, an itinerant player, records in his journal the performance of an original play "on the Subject of the Country." This unknown work may have been the first American play.

1714   Robert Hunter's *Androboros* becomes the first play to be published in America.

1750   The General Court of Massachusetts passes "An Act to Prevent Stage-Plays, and other Theatrical Entertainment."

1766   *Ponteach*, a play by Major Robert Rogers, is printed. Although it was probably never acted, it is the best of the early plays dealing with the Indian problem.

1767 Thomas Godfrey's *The Prince of Parthia* is acted in Philadelphia on April 24, thus becoming the first play by a native American to be produced professionally in this country.

1774 The First Continental Congress issues a declaration opposing "shews, plays, and other expensive diversions and entertainments," effectively bringing to a close the first period of American drama.

1775 Mercy Otis Warren's satiric farce *The Group* is published. It is the best of the Revolutionary "pamphlet plays."

1787 Royall Tyler's comedy, *The Contrast*, is acted in New York on April 16, thus becoming the first comedy by a native American to be produced professionally in this country.

1789 William Dunlap's *The Father; or, American Shandyism* is acted in New York on September 7. This is the second native comedy to be produced and the play that launches the career of the "Father of the American Drama."

1797 John Daly Burk's drama *Bunker-Hill*, best of the Revolutionary patriotic dramas, is acted on February 17 in Boston.

1798 Dunlap's *André*, America's first tragedy on a native theme, is acted on March 30 at New York's Park Theatre. It remains the finest of Dunlap's plays.

1806 John Howard Payne's first play, *Julia; or, The Wanderer*, is produced on February 7 at the Park. Payne, later to become an actor-dramatist of international repute, is fourteen years old at the time.

1819 Mordecai Manuel Noah's *She Would Be a Soldier*, the most popular of the early patriotic comedies, is acted on June 21 at the Park.

1824 James Nelson Barker's historical tragedy *Superstition* is acted on March 12 in Philadelphia. It is generally considered the finest American play from the first quarter of the nineteenth century.

On May 27, Payne's *Charles the Second* is first acted at London's Covent Garden. A collaboration with Washington Irving, this is the best of Payne's plays.

1831   Robert Montgomery Bird's drama *The Gladiator* is first acted by Edwin Forrest in New York on September 26, marking the beginning of a six-year collaboration of Bird and Forrest.

1834   Bird's finest play, *The Broker of Bogota*, is first acted by Forrest on February 12 in New York.

1841   Dion Boucicault's comedy of manners *London Assurance* is first acted at Covent Garden on March 4, launching the career of this most successful international dramatist.

1845   Anna Cora Mowatt's *Fashion*, the finest American comedy of manners of the nineteenth century, premieres on March 24 in New York.

1855   George Henry Boker's *Francesca da Rimini*, the finest American tragedy of the nineteenth century, is first acted on September 26 in New York.

1856   Congress passes a Copyright Law offering some degree of protection for the American dramatist, thanks largely to the efforts of Boker and Boucicault.

1859   Boucicault's *The Octoroon*, one of the better American melodramas, premieres on December 5 in New York.

1867   Augustin Daly's melodrama *Under the Gaslight* is first acted on August 12 in New York. Its immense popularity depends in part upon its "tied-to-the-railroad-tracks" climax.

1879   David Belasco and James A. Herne begin a playwriting collaboration that results in *Chums*, later retitled *Hearts of Oak*, a success that launches Herne's career as a major American dramatist.

1882   Belasco's first Broadway play opens at Wallack's Theatre on May 8. *La Belle Russe* is the first of 123 Broadway productions in which Belasco is to be involved during his long career as producer-playwright.

1887   Bronson Howard's *The Henrietta*, representing a major advance toward realism in the American theater, opens on September 26 in New York. *The Henrietta* firmly establishes the reputation of Howard, who is later to be called the "Dean of the American drama."

1889   The revised version of Howard's *Shenandoah*, the most successful of all Civil War dramas, opens on September 9 in New York.

1890   James A. Herne's great realistic domestic tragedy, *Margaret Fleming*, premieres in Lynn, Massachusetts, on July 4.

1891   The American Dramatists Club, forerunner of the Dramatists' Guild, is founded by Bronson Howard.

The United States accepts the International Copyright Agreement, offering greater legal protection for the American dramatist.

Unable to attract a producer, Herne himself restages *Margaret Fleming* at Chickering Hall, Boston, on May 4. This performance is considered the beginning of the Free Theatre movement in America.

1892   Herne's *Shore Acres*, the success of which is eventually to make Herne a millionaire, premieres in Chicago on May 23.

1895   Belasco's very successful Civil War drama, *The Heart of Maryland*, premieres in Washington, D.C., on October 9.

1905   Belasco's highly successful melodrama of the West, *The Girl of the Golden West*, premieres in Pittsburgh on October 3. It is to become the source play for Puccini's opera *La Fanciulla del West*.

1911   *The Return of Peter Grimm*, probably Belasco's finest play, premieres in Boston on January 2.

PREFACE

There are those who maintain that no drama of any worth was written in America before the appearance of Eugene O'Neill (1888–1953)—an extreme posture, of course, but one that attests to the average reader's lack of familiarity with early American drama. Every schoolboy and schoolgirl learns about Cooper and Hawthorne, about Longfellow and Melville and Mark Twain. But the names of William Dunlap or Royall Tyler, of John Howard Payne or Robert Montgomery Bird or Anna Cora Mowatt Ritchie, are unknown to them.

Few readers—even habitual theatergoers—consider that America has a heritage in dramatic literature as well as in poetry and fiction. For some reason, the image of our eighteenth-century forebears sitting in the playhouse seldom comes to mind. Yet there were playwrights and plays and theatergoers on the North American continent almost from the time the first settlers stepped off their boats.

The reason for this lack of familiarity with America's early drama is plain: probably no single American play from the late eighteenth or nineteenth centuries can be called a masterpiece of dramatic literature. Viewed as a body of work, however, the early American drama says much about the nation's founders and early citizens—about their political and social concerns and their attitudes toward their new nation as it struggled to emerge and prosper, independent of its European cousins. Moreover, there are some early American plays of genuine artistic and literary merit, plays that can hold their own in comparison with the mainstream of the British and European drama that was produced at the same time. It is upon these plays, and the men and women who wrote them, that this work focuses.

Naturally, the subject of early American drama is a vast one for a volume of this size, and limits must, of necessity, be observed. The present discussion begins with the earliest record of dramatic activity in North America and progresses chronologically to roughly the close of the nineteenth century. Therefore, no attempt has been made to include every important dramatist. The essays are selective, most chapters focusing upon a limited number of playwrights who may be considered representative either of their time or of a particular movement—for example, "Dramatists of the Revolution," "The Romantic Movement," "The Move Toward Realism," and so on. Three of the dramatists discussed have been considered of sufficient importance to warrant a full chapter each.

Some twenty dramatists are discussed in varying detail, as are approximately forty plays. It is hoped that the reader will discover in these necessarily cursory examinations of early American plays and playwrights a sense of the overall development of the American drama. If the reader finds his interest engaged to the point of pursuing further reading on the dramatists, or even of turning to the texts of the plays themselves, this volume will have served its purpose.

1. GENESIS

The Colonial Period

It seems ironic that our earliest account of English-language theatrical activity on the North American continent should be one concerned with prohibition and litigation, for the American theater was to be plagued by censorship and judicial proscription until well after the Revolution. On August 27, 1665, one William Darby and two confederates were called into a Virginia court to answer charges of having performed (and presumably written) a play called *Ye Bare and Ye Cubb*. The judge required them to appear in costume and recite portions of the work. Their command performance must have been persuasive, for His Honor acquitted the trio and ordered the plaintiff, one Edward Martin, to pay the court costs.

Whether *Ye Bare and Ye Cubb* was truly the first American play we will never know, just as we will never know what there was about it that so offended Edward Martin. But the account does illustrate the pervasive prejudice against plays and players felt by the early American settlers. All of the colonies except Virginia and Maryland enacted legislation prohibiting theatrical performances. Typical of such laws were those in Pennsylvania and New York. The Assembly of Pennsylvania in 1700 banned "stage plays, masks, revels" and other "rude and riotous sports," and in 1709 the Governor's Council of New York forbade "play acting and prize fighting." Most colonies had similar edicts in force at one time or another.

The city most doggedly antitheater was Boston. In March of 1750 the General Court of Massachusetts passed "An Act to Prevent Stage-Plays, and other Theatrical Entertainment," a law that remained in force and was reenacted in 1784. Such legislation created a climate hardly conducive to the rapid development of native dramatic literature, yet the drama did evolve and the theater, that "fabulous invalid," managed to remain alive.

One reason for its survival in the face of so much legal prohibition was the determination and ingenuity of the actors. David Douglass, for example, cunningly circumvented the Rhode Island law in 1761 by advertising his production of *Othello* as a "Series of Moral Dialogues in five parts depicting the evil effects of jealousy and other Sad Passions and Proving that Happiness can only spring from the Pursuit of Virtue."

Then, too, dramatic activity was promoted and encouraged on the amateur level in America's colonial colleges. Most of these early college performances were in the nature of commemorative odes and dialogues rather than fully developed plays. One of the earliest of such productions was a "pastoral colloquy" presented at the College of William and Mary in 1702. Through the performance of these odes and dialogues, the colonial colleges helped to generate and nurture the histrionic impulse in their students. Such activity was, nevertheless, strictly amateur.

Professional dramatic activity in the American colonies can be traced back to an entry in the journal of Anthony Aston, an itinerant English player. Chronicling his activities for 1703, Aston wrote at one point:

"We arriv'd in Charles-Town, full of Lice, Shame, Poverty, Nakedness and Hunger. I turned Player and Poet, and wrote one Play on the Subject of the Country." Aston's play may have been the first professional performance in America of a play written in this country, but we know nothing of it.

Evidence of dramatic activity becomes more substantial, of course, in the case of those plays that reached print and have been preserved. There are a surprising number of such plays, few of which were ever acted. The first play to be published in America was *Androboros, a Biographical Farce in Three Acts* (1714) by Robert Hunter (d. 1734). Hunter was an Englishman who served as royal governor in New York and New Jersey from 1710 to 1719 and as governor of Jamaica from 1729 to his death. He was a writer of some note in his time, being much admired by Jonathan Swift, and he used playwriting as a vehicle for satire and as an outlet for his personal political frustration, as did many of the early American dramatists.

Androboros (Man-Eater) is a bawdy satire whose main target was Hunter's obstructionist lieutenant governor, General Francis Nicholson. Of the play's fifteen characters, in fact, thirteen can be identified as figures in New York politics. Amazingly enough, Hunter succeeded, through publication of his satire, in silencing his political opponents and quelling the divisiveness with which he had been forced to contend because of Nicholson.

Androboros was never produced, and for good reasons according to one critic, who noted that the "plot turns on so filthy an incident as to preclude its performance, even in the coarse and vulgar time of its writing."[1] The "filthy incident" is some scatological horseplay in which one character's gown is to be "Beskirted and Besh——," in order to discredit the supposed offender, who will be easily identified by the "Size and Colour of the T——." This excremental humor runs throughout *Androboros*, but the farce is nonetheless an incisive and genuinely humorous satire.[2]

No American plays have survived from the fifty-year period following the printing of *Androboros*, although it is certain that plays were written and staged in those years. Our next surviving text is *The Paxton Boys*, published anonymously in 1764. Like *Androboros*, it is satiric in intent and is not suitable for the stage. The butts of its satire are the Pennsylvania Presbyterians and Episcopalians, and the central issue is the frontier settlers' ineptitude in dealing with the Indian problem.

The American Indian was portrayed in a number of early American dramas, one of the first of which was *Le Père-Indien*, known to have been performed by amateurs in New Orleans in 1753. The play, which has not survived, was written by LeBlanc de Villeneuve, a French officer, and dealt with the Choctaw Indians, who were its heroes. Villeneuve reputedly wrote a tragedy as well: *Poucha-Houmma*, based on an Indian story.

The best of the Indian plays from the colonial period is *Ponteach; or, The Savages of America*, written by Major Robert Rogers (1731–1795) and published in London in 1766. It has been called America's first tragedy on a native subject, but it was never acted. Rogers was born in Massachusetts and lived on the New Hampshire frontier. He fought in the French and Indian War, but his career as a military man was not without blemish; he was accused of being involved in illicit trade with the Indians. He traveled to England a number of times and died there at the age of sixty-four.

Rogers knew Ponteach (pronounced Pontiac) personally and had firsthand knowledge of Indian trading, a fact that endows his romantic tragedy with some significance as a historical document, if not as a great piece of literature. *Ponteach* combines romance with social commentary as it exposes the ruthlessness of the white man's dealings with the noble savage. Ponteach is a heroic figure who is victimized and ultimately defeated in battle by the English. The play was to serve as a model for scores of subsequent plays extolling the nobility of the American aborigine.

It is worth noting that colonial America produced at least one female dramatist, Charlotte Ramsay Lennox (1720–1804), who was born in America but lived in England from the age of fifteen. She was a personal friend of Oliver Goldsmith and Dr. Johnson, and she became an actress after 1748. Her comedy *The Sister* failed at Covent Garden in 1769 but was translated into German in 1776, thus becoming the first play by a native American to be translated into a foreign language.

By 1767, colonial America still had not seen a play by a native son or daughter professionally produced on one of its stages, but it appeared that such an event was about to occur. The Pennsylvania *Chronicle* of April 6, 1767, carried an advertisement for the American Company, which was then playing in Philadelphia's Southwark Theatre. The article announced a performance of *The Disappointment; or, The Force of Credulity*, to be given on April 20. The play, published that same year under the pseudonym of Andrew Barton, was by Thomas Forrest, a native Pennsylvanian who later became a colonel in the Revolutionary forces.

The Disappointment, America's first ballad-opera, is a satiric burlesque of Philadelphia political personalities. It is the first play to utilize the song "Yankee Doodle," the first to present the stereotype of the stage Irishman, and perhaps the first to include a Negro character in dialect. It would have made a fitting beginning for a truly American drama, had it not been suddenly withdrawn from production. A notice in the Pennsylvania *Gazette* for April 16 announced the disappointment that *The Disappointment* would not be presented, due to its "personal reflections," which made it "unfit for the stage."[3]

Thus, Forrest's satiric opera lost the distinction of being the first play by a native American to be produced professionally in America, and that honor passed to Thomas Godfrey's *The Prince of Parthia*, acted four days later on April 24, 1767. This is, in a sense, unfortunate, for Godfrey's classical tragedy is perhaps of less interest to the student of Americana than *The Disappointment*.

America's First Tragedy

The Prince of Parthia reflects both the callowness and the classical schooling of its author, Thomas Godfrey. Godfrey was born December 4, 1736, and had finished writing *The Prince of Parthia*, his first and only drama, by 1759 at the latest—by the age of twenty-two. The play, although highly imitative of various earlier works, did show promise—a promise that, unfortunately, was never to be realized, for Godfrey died four years later, on August 3, 1763, at the age of twenty-six.

Godfrey was the son of Thomas Godfrey, inventor of the sea quadrant. The elder Godfrey died when his son was thirteen, and the boy was apprenticed to a watchmaker. In that position he might have remained, had he not been released from his indentures by William Smith, provost of the College of Philadelphia, who saw in the boy some potential for scholarship. Smith was a patron of the arts and especially of the theater. Under his tutelage Godfrey gained exposure to art and culture, having as his fellow students such young men as Benjamin West, soon to become America's foremost painter, and Francis Hopkinson, who later distinguished himself in the Congress.

Godfrey's study with Provost Smith brought him into contact with the theater, and he probably attended performances of the Hallam company in their 1754 Philadelphia season. Godfrey also may have participated in the college's production of *The Masque of Alfred* during the Christmas holidays of 1756–57. It may indeed have been that experience that inspired him to begin work on *The Prince of Parthia*.

Thomas Godfrey's literary interests were not confined to the drama. A poet of some accomplishment, he contributed verse to the *American Magazine* several times in 1758. His major poetic work was *The Court of Fancy* (1762), written in a style imitative of Chaucer and of Pope.

In May of 1758 Godfrey was commissioned an ensign in the Pennsylvania militia and took part in the expedition against Fort Duquesne, after which he was promoted to lieutenant. He lived chiefly in Wilmington, North Carolina, after 1759, and it is there that he died of a violent fever. He was, according to one recent commentator, an "outstanding dramatist for his time with a potential denied only by his early death."[4]

The Prince of Parthia is an extremely derivative, five-act romantic tragedy that recalls the heroic tragedy of the English Restoration period, the classical tragedy of the eighteenth century, and, most unmistakably, the tragedies of Shakespeare. Its plot is almost entirely Godfrey's invention, but the language that conveys it calls to mind one Shakespeare passage after another.

Parthia was a country in West Asia (now a part of Iran) during early Christian times, but Godfrey drew upon Parthian history only slightly and then principally for his characters' names. Arsaces (the generic term for a Parthian ruler) is the play's hero and one of three sons to King Artabanus, the other two being Vardanes, the villain of the piece, and Gotarzes, a noble youth who ultimately becomes king.

The play opens with the triumphal return to Parthia of Arsaces, who has defeated the Arabians. Immediately we see that Arsaces is hated by his jealous brother Vardanes "for standing 'twixt him, and the hope of Empire," and by the Queen, Artabanus' second wife, whose treacherous son Arsaces had earlier slain in battle. We next meet Evanthe, an Arabian princess held captive in Parthia, who loves Arsaces and is loved by both Vardanes and the King. Arsaces has brought back in chains a captive, Bethas, the Arabian king and, unbeknownst to Arsaces, the father of Evanthe. Arsaces pleads for his noble captive's life and the King grants it, sentencing the unfortunate Bethas to prison.

The second act shows the nobility of Arsaces as he visits Bethas, his former enemy and captive, in his cell and befriends him. Evanthe then appears at the prison, bringing about a tearful reunion of father and daughter. Arsaces, deeply moved by the scene, vows to plead with his father for the release of Bethas and for the hand of Evanthe in marriage.

The third act opens with the Queen complaining that the King has abandoned her bed because of his infatuation for the captive Evanthe. A passionate argument between the royal couple ensues, after which the Queen cunningly tells Vardanes that his own father is his rival for the love of Evanthe. This prompts Vardanes to plot the destruction of both Arsaces and the King. He tells the latter that Arsaces is conspiring to join with Bethas in the overthrow of the kingdom, which prompts the King to order Arsaces' arrest and imprisonment.

Act IV opens with the rather surprising announce-

ment that King Artabanus is dead, slain by Vardanes'
accomplice, Lysias. Vardanes seems at this point to
have disposed of his father and his brother rather
nicely. The Queen comes to Arsaces' cell to stab him
but is prevented when the ghost of the King intervenes and drives her mad. In the final scene of the act,
Arsaces is freed by his brother Gotarzes, who has
joined forces with the leader of an invading army,
Barzaphernes. The three decide to wage war against
Vardanes and restore Arsaces to his rightful place as
the King of Parthia.

Meanwhile, Vardanes confronts Evanthe and attempts to seduce her by promising to spare Arsaces
if she will yield to him. When this fails, he attempts a
rape but is prevented by the news of Arsaces' escape
and the imminent attack. An offstage battle between
the opposing forces of Vardanes and Arsaces is nar-
rated to Evanthe by her confidante, Cleone, who mis-
takes one Phraates for Arsaces and reports wrongly
that the prince has been slain. Evanthe, not surprisingly, is grief-stricken. In the final scene, Arsaces' victory celebration is cut short when Evanthe, who has
taken poison, is led in. She has time only to realize her
mistake, bid farewell to her beloved Arsaces, and ex-
pire. Arsaces runs mad with grief and stabs himself,
and the play ends with Gotarzes assuming the throne
of Parthia.

Godfrey's debt to Shakespeare is obvious in a number of episodes, as well as in several passages of dialogue that paraphrase Shakespeare's verse. Godfrey's
opening scene, in which Gotarzes and Phraates de-
scribe Arsaces' triumphal return, recalls the opening
of *Julius Caesar*. Vardanes describes the cheering
Parthians:

> The houses' tops
> With gaping spectators are throng'd, nay wild

They climb such precipices that the eye
Is dazzl'd with their darings.

Shakespeare's Romans, cheering Caesar, were similarly
described:

Many a time and oft
Have you climb'd up to walls and battlements,
To towers and windows, yea, to chimney-tops . . .

Vardanes also rebukes the Parthian masses for the
same sort of fickleness that Shakespeare dramatized in
his Roman crowds.

Other echoes of *Julius Caesar* occur in *The Prince
of Parthia*. We learn that Arsaces had earlier saved
Vardanes from drowning, just as Cassius had once res-
cued Caesar. Arsaces cries out, at one point: "Ye fig-
ur'd stones!/Ye senseless, lifeless images of men" (II,
vii), recalling Marullus's "You blocks, you stones, you
worse than senseless things" (*Caesar*, I, i). And when
Vardanes plots his conspiracy against Arsaces:

The Heav'ns appear as one continu'd flame,
Earth with her terror shakes, dim night retires,
And the red lightning gives a dreadful day,
While in the thunder's voice each sound is lost.
(II, ii)

In like fashion does stormy nature presage the assassination of Caesar in the Shakespeare play (*Caesar*, II, ii).

Godfrey's play produces echoes as well of *King
Lear*, *Hamlet*, and *Romeo and Juliet*. Vardanes turns
his father against Arsaces (III, viii) with precisely the
same stratagem (a feigned letter) that Edmund uses
against Edgar (*Lear*, I, ii), and the reunion of Bethas
and Evanthe (II, vii) is modeled after that of Lear and
Cordelia (*Lear*, IV, vii). *Hamlet* is imitated in the
visitation of Artabanus' ghost to the Queen (IV, v), a

variation on the Hamlet–Gertrude–Ghost episode of Shakespeare's play (*Hamlet*, III, iv), although the Queen paraphrases Macbeth in confronting the specter: "Why dost thou shake thy horrid locks at me?" ("Never shake/Thy gory locks at me" [*Macbeth*, III, iv]). Finally, *Romeo and Juliet* is strongly suggested in the ending of Godfrey's tragedy, where the lovers' suicide results from misunderstanding and poor timing.

Were it not for its reliance upon earlier models, *The Prince of Parthia* might be considered a rather effective tragedy for its time. It is certainly as well conceived and as well constructed as the bulk of serious plays produced in England during the mid-eighteenth century. Godfrey was meticulous in his plotting, and there are fleeting poetic passages of genuine merit.

It is all the more unfortunate, therefore, that *The Prince of Parthia* has no relevance to American political or social concerns of the time. It would take some imagination, for example, to credit Godfrey with creating in King Artabanus a dramatic portrait of George III, although Bethas tells the Parthian ruler:

> Trust not too much, vain Monarch, to your pow'r,
> Know fortune places all her choicest gifts
> On ticklish heights, they shake with ev'ry breeze,
> And oft some rude wind hurls them to the ground.
> . . . .
> What King can boast, to morrow as to day,
> Thus, happy will I reign?

The Prince of Parthia seems far removed from colonial America, yet it must claim the title of "America's first tragedy." In the words of Arthur Hobson Quinn, noted historian of the American drama: "It was a product of the dramatic impulses of the time, deliberately written not only for the stage but also for the company that performed it, and it remains, therefore, in a special sense the representative play of its period."[5]

Dramatists of the Revolution

By 1774, relations between the American colonies and the British crown had deteriorated to the point that war seemed imminent. The colonists convened the First Continental Congress in Philadelphia on September 5, and the Congress took steps to prepare the citizenry. One such step was the issuance of a declaration discouraging "every species of extravagance and dissipation, especially all horse-racing, and all kinds of gaming, cock-fighting, exhibitions of shews, plays, and other expensive diversions and entertainments." Even though the declaration did not have the force of law, it effectively brought to an end the production of plays in the Colonies. Thus, the curtain fell on the first period of American theatrical history.

The congressional proscription did not, however, put an end to the writing of plays in the Colonies, and the Revolutionary period proved to be a fertile one for the drama—especially for short, satiric "pamphlet plays" espousing one political viewpoint or another. Few of these plays were intended for production but they reached print with amazing swiftness and have survived as documentary evidence of the intensity of political sentiment during the war years. Written by both the colonists and the British, they expressed both Patriot and Loyalist viewpoints. By literary standards, they are weak in plot and characterization, being intended principally to persuade their readers to one side or another by satirizing real persons and events. The best of the writers of these pamphlets was a woman, Mercy Otis Warren (1728–1814).

Mercy Otis, born in Barnstable, Massachusetts, was

the third of thirteen children. Her brother James Otis was himself a pamphleteer in the Patriot cause during the 1760s and a statesman of some repute. In 1754, Mercy married James Warren, who later became President of the Provincial Congress and a general in Washington's army. Mrs. Warren was well read, intelligent, and very much aware of the political activity surrounding her. She was a good friend to the leaders of the day, especially Samuel Adams, Thomas Jefferson, and John Adams, with whose wife she shared a special friendship. Writing of Mercy Warren, John Adams once praised the "classical Satyr, such as flows so naturally & easily from the pen of my excellent Friend,"[6] and he wrote at another time that her "poetical pen" had "no equal that I know of in this country."[7]

Although she never saw a play on the stage, Mercy Warren read Shakespeare and Molière and had an instinctive gift for the satiric mode. At least five satiric farces have been attributed to her, but only two can be proven hers with complete certainty: *The Adulateur* and *The Group*.

The Adulateur, a Tragedy, As it is now acted in Upper Servia was published in 1773 with no authorship indicated. It had appeared earlier, also anonymously, in two installments in the Massachusetts *Spy* for March and April, 1772. The 1773 version is a five-act play, but Mrs. Warren repudiated the final two acts as a "plagiary" by some "unknown hand." *The Adulateur* is a satiric attack upon Thomas Hutchinson, the colonial governor of Massachusetts, who is revealed, under the character name of Rapatio, as a hypocritical despot and a stooge of the British government. James Otis, Mrs. Warren's brother, appears in the sympathetic character of Brutus.

The best known of Mercy Warren's pamphlet plays is *The Group*, written early in 1775 and published anonymously that same year. The Group of the title was a coterie of sixteen men who made up the Massachusetts Council, a governing body appointed by royal mandate in abrogation of the Charter of Massachusetts. Mercy Warren and other Patriot sympathizers saw the council as a violation of their right to elective government and viewed its sixteen members as virtual traitors.

In Mrs. Warren's play, the members of the Group express varying degrees of contempt for the Massachusetts colonists. Most violent is Hateall (Timothy Ruggles, a Tory), who curses the Patriots and swears:

> Compassion ne'er shall seize my steadfast breast
> Though blood and carnage spread thro' all the
> land;
> Till streaming purple tinge the verdant turf,
> Till ev'ry street shall float with human gore,
> I Nero-like, the capital in flames,
> Could laugh to see her glotted sons expire,
> Tho' much too rough my soul to touch the lyre.
>
> (I, i)

Although Hutchinson had, by the time of *The Group*, left the colony, he too is remembered in the play, when Collateralis (Judge William Broune) says of Rapatio:

> Can you suppose there yet is such a dupe
> As still believes that wretch an honest man?
> The later strokes of his serpentine brain
> Outvie the arts of Machiavel himself,
> His Borgian model here is realiz'd
> And the stale tricks of politicians play'd
> Beneath a vizard fair.
>
> (II, i)

Mercy Warren's satire is strong stuff, but the play itself, like most of the political pamphlet plays of its time, is not stageworthy, being essentially composed of conversations rather than dramatic action. Moreover, much of the point of *The Group* is lost on a modern reader unless he is familiar with the persons and situations under attack. Still, *The Group* is a significant and interesting historical document. Quinn termed it an "outcry of democracy against oligarchy, of liberty against prerogative, of the descendant of the Puritans against the upholders of kingcraft and oppression."[8]

The other pamphlet plays sometimes attributed to Mercy Warren are *The Defeat* (1773), which also ridicules Hutchinson as Rapatio; *The Blockheads; or, The Affrighted Officers* (1776), a lampoon of General Burgoyne, written in a style too vulgar for Mrs. Warren's pen, and *The Motley Assembly* (1779), a one-act farce that satirizes social behavior. Mercy Otis Warren also wrote two rather dull and lengthy tragedies, *The Ladies of Castile* and *The Sack of Rome*, published together in *Poems, Dramatic and Miscellaneous* (1790). Her *History of the Rise, Progress and Termination of the American Revolution*, completed in 1805, is a three-volume work of considerable accomplishment and historical value.

Political satire was not the only type of drama written in the war years. Patriotic plays on contemporary events found a receptive readership and served to chronicle the progress of the Revolution. One such play of special significance is *The Fall of British Tyranny; or, American Liberty Triumphant*, written early in 1776 by John Leacock (1729–1802; cited in some sources as Joseph Leacock). Leacock was a gold- and silversmith, later a farmer, and a prominent Philadelphian. He was a member (perhaps founder) of the Patriot Society of the Sons of St. Tammany and a tolerable poet as well as a dramatist.

The Fall of British Tyranny may be considered

America's first chronicle play. It is a sprawling, epic prose drama chronicling the development of the Revolutionary War. It sports a large cast, five acts, and twenty-five scenes; its settings include locales in both England and America. Leacock wrote the play to inspire the American people during the Revolution, and it was quite popular with its readers. It may even have been staged. *The Fall of British Tyranny* is the first play to include George Washington as a dramatic character.

Hugh Henry Brackenridge (1748–1816) also made important contributions to the drama of the Revolutionary period. Born in Scotland, Brackenridge was reared in Pennsylvania and became a teacher in Maryland and New Jersey, pursuing careers also as a judge, a legislator, and a minister. He is perhaps best remembered by literary historians as the author of *Modern Chivalry* (1792), a collection of satiric sketches and stories. He also wrote a number of odes and elegies.

Brackenridge's two plays, *The Battle of Bunker's Hill* (1776) and *The Death of General Montgomery* (1777), are fairly unusual for their time in that they are not satiric in nature but are serious attempts at historical reporting, with an emphasis on character development. He wrote them as exercises for his students at the Maryland Academy, and they are essentially declamatory conversations rather than theatrical pieces. Both are extremely "narrative," the action taking place off stage and being only reported, and both are fervently patriotic, extolling bravery and heroism in the face of defeat. Brackenridge's plays did much to bolster the Patriots' spirits in times when the failure of the Revolution seemed imminent.

The plays of Mercy Warren, Leacock, and Brackenridge were either bitterly satiric or unrelievedly somber, but there was one Revolutionary dramatist at least who courted the comic muse: Robert Munford

(1737?–1783). Munford was a Virginia planter who had been educated in England, and his two plays, *The Candidates* and *The Patriots*, are reminiscent of late-eighteenth-century English comedy, anticipating the style of Royall Tyler's *The Contrast*, which was to be produced in 1787. Although Munford's plays were not published until 1798, they were written in the 1770s and are, surprisingly, nonpolitical.

Munford was, perhaps, the best of the Revolutionary dramatists in his attention to plotting and dramatic structure. His two comedies, unlike their contemporaries, are quite stageworthy. *The Candidates*, a farcical satire on Virginia election practices, is noteworthy for including the character of Ralpho, a Negro. *The Patriots* focuses on romantic entanglements and nicely handles three love intrigues simultaneously. It has, as well, pacifist overtones.

Munford has been termed America's first comic dramatist, but the appellation is somewhat misplaced in view of the fact that neither of his plays was produced on stage. Thus, the label of "America's first comedy" is conventionally bestowed upon a play that was to appear well after the war had ended and the new American nation had been established: *The Contrast* by Royall Tyler.

2. AMERICA'S FIRST COMEDY

Critics and historians have shown some confusion regarding the exact label that should attach to *The Contrast* by Royall Tyler (1757–1826), calling it variously "the first American play," "America's first play with a native subject," "the first American play to be produced," and other attributions—all inaccurate. What *The Contrast* is, in truth, is the first comedy by a native American to be produced professionally in America. It also bears the distinction of being the first American play to be reviewed in the press.

Royall Tyler was born July 18, 1757, to Royall and Mary Steele Tyler of Boston. He was christened William Clark, but his mother had his name legally changed to Royall shortly after his father's death. Tyler's family was one of some means and the youth was given a traditional seven-year education at Latin School, after which he entered Harvard on July 15, 1772, just before his fifteenth birthday.

Tyler was a handsome, popular, and somewhat mischievous student at Harvard, a school that exacted rigorous standards of conduct from its students. One of the college's many rules seems particularly ironic today, in view of Tyler's later connection with the theater. It read in part:

> If any Undergraduate shall presume to be an Actor in, a Spectator at, or any Ways concerned in any Stage Plays, Interludes or Theatrical Entertainments in the Town of Cambridge or elsewhere, he shall for the first Offence be degraded—& for any repeated Offence shall be rusticated or expelled.[1]

The rule did not preclude participation in debate or oratory, however, and it was in those activities that Tyler developed the speaking skills that were to serve him so well in his career as an attorney and later as a judge.

Tyler received his B.A. degree from Harvard in July of 1776, shortly after the signing of the Declaration of Independence, and received a like degree simultaneously from Yale, *honoris causa*. He embarked immediately upon the study of law and, after a brief military career in the Battle of Rhode Island under the command of John Hancock, received his M.A. degree from Harvard in 1779. He was admitted to the bar in 1780.

The accounts of Tyler's personal life are sketchy, but some evidence suggests that he was given somewhat to frivolity and dissipation as a young man. A particularly interesting account is that of his courtship of John Adams's daughter Abigail. Tyler courted "Nabby" Adams for about two years, during which time her father was abroad and knew of the affair only through letters from his wife. Adams was at first strongly opposed to Tyler's interest in his daughter, writing of the young man as a "reformed Rake" and a "youth who has been giddy enough to spend his Fortune or half his Fortune in Gaieties."[2] Although Adams later altered his opinion of Tyler and allowed the affair to advance, Tyler evidently lost interest in the girl and in 1785 the Adams–Tyler alliance ended. Tyler eventually married Mary Hunt Palmer in 1794.

We will never know precisely what sort of "Gaieties" the young Royall Tyler indulged himself in. They may have been no more than postgraduate high spirits, for there is no other evidence to suggest that Tyler was anything but a hardworking and dedicated attorney. His distinguished career in law itself attests to his seriousness of purpose. In July of 1783 he was sworn in as an attorney of the Supreme Judicial Court, and he served as State's Attorney for Windham County for seven years, beginning in 1794. In 1801 he was elected as one of three judges of the Vermont Supreme Court, and he was Chief Justice from 1807 until 1813. He was, as well, a trustee of the University of Vermont from 1802 to 1813 and Professor of Jurisprudence there from 1811 to 1814. Throughout his career, Tyler was an outstanding attorney and a highly respected judge, noted for his impartiality and his persuasive oratory.

Literature was, for Royall Tyler, an avocation and it remained so, in spite of the reputation he earned for his literary works. He began to contribute verse to various periodicals as early as 1793 and continued to publish poetry until 1807. With Joseph Dennie as his partner, he coauthored the famous "Colon & Spondee" columns, satiric essays in literary criticism that appeared in various journals beginning in 1794. The Colon & Spondee articles were widely imitated and are considered today a highpoint in early American journalism. Tyler is recognized by literary historians also for his two-volume picaresque novel, *The Algerine Captive*, published in 1797.

Royall Tyler's association with the theater began as the fortuitous result of a military assignment. He had served as an aide to General Lincoln in the attempt to capture the insurgents in Shays' Rebellion from Janu-

The Contrast. The foppish Mr. Dimple, periwig awry, is ridiculed in the comedy's final scene. Produced by California State University Dominguez Hills for the American Bicentennial. Directed by Jack Vaughn; designed by Peter Lach.
RICHARD RUTLEDGE

ary through March of 1787; in connection with that mission he was sent to New York on March 12. It was his first visit to that city. By April 16 his first play, *The Contrast*, had been performed at the John Street Theatre by the Old American Company.

Although he had undoubtedly read plays, it is unlikely that Tyler had ever seen a play on stage before his 1787 visit to New York. Upon his arrival there, however, he could have seen *Much Ado About Nothing*, *Cymbeline*, *Richard III*, Garrick's *The Clandestine Marriage*, Colman's *The Jealous Wife*, and—most importantly—Sheridan's *The School for Scandal* on March 21, a play that strongly influenced his writing of *The Contrast*.

Tyler's first play was an instant success. Writing under the byline of "Candour" in the *Daily Advertiser* for April 18, a reviewer called it the "production of a man of genius" and labeled its sentiments the "effusions of an honest patriot heart expressed with energy and eloquence." The play was repeated on April 18 and on May 2 and 12, an astonishing number of performances for any new play in that period. *The Contrast* was staged subsequently in Baltimore and Philadelphia, and in Boston, where it was advertised as a "Moral Lecture in five parts." In all, there is evidence of at least thirty-eight performances of *The Contrast* by the Old American Company between 1787 and 1804; there were various productions by other companies as well.

Whether Tyler wrote *The Contrast* entirely in the five-week period between his March 12 arrival in New York and the play's premiere, as has often been claimed, we will never know. But it is obvious that he was a fast worker when it came to dramatic composition. His second play, *May Day in Town; or, New York in an Uproar*, was ready for a May 19 opening, also at the John Street Theatre. *May Day in Town*, a comic opera, was not so successful as *The Contrast*, earning but a single performance. Unfortunately, the work has not survived.

A decade after *The Contrast* and *May Day in Town*, Tyler was to have two other plays produced professionally, neither of which has survived. The first, *The Farm House; or, The Female Duellists*, was presented in Boston on May 6, 1796, and may have been an adaptation of John Philip Kemble's *The Farm House* (1789). The second, somewhat more success-ful, was *The Georgia Spec; or, Land in the Moon*, presumably a satire on land speculation in Georgia's Yazoo County. It played in Boston on October 30, 1797, and in New York on December 20 and 23 and on February 12, 1798. There is also sketchy evidence of a Tyler adaptation of Molière's *The Doctor in Spite of Himself* (ca. 1795) and of a play he wrote for children called *Five Pumpkins*, but neither is extant.

Aside from *The Contrast*, we have the texts of only four other plays by Royall Tyler, none of which was produced on the stage. The best of the four is *The Island of Barrataria* [*sic*], a three-act prose farce based on the Barataria episodes in Cervantes' *Don Quixote*. The other three are sacred-verse dramas based on Old Testament stories: *The Judgement of Solomon, The Origin of the Feast of Purim*, and *Joseph and His Brethren*.[3]

Royall Tyler contributed much to the emerging American nation, promoting respect for its laws and enhancing its literature, but his final years were not happy ones. He left public service in 1813, from which time he began to suffer from a facial cancer that was eventually to claim his life. From 1822 on, he and his wife were reduced to virtual poverty, living on public charity as his illness advanced. He died at Brattleboro on August 26, 1826.

The Contrast

In the third act of *The Contrast*, the Yankee plowboy, Jonathan, tells of attending the theater and seeing a play performed—a play he calls "The School for Scandalization." The reference is, of course, to Richard Brinsley Sheridan's *The School for Scandal* (1777), a comedy that Tyler had obviously seen in New York on March 21, three and a half weeks before *The Contrast* was performed. It is a telling reference, for Tyler's comedy closely imitates the features of mid-eighteenth-century English comedy of manners, and the imitation, although it is distinctly American, is an admirable one.

The "Contrast" of the title is that between European affectation and American plain dealing, and Tyler lost no opportunity to point up the difference. The play's cast of characters illustrates the "contrast" theme, with each major figure set into strong relief by a character of opposite nature. The leading lady is Miss Charolotte Manly, a gay coquette whose flightiness is contrasted to her sober and sentimental friend Maria, whom Charlotte calls a "dear little piece of old fashioned prudery" (I, i).

Both women are courted by the traveled and English-bred Billy Dimple, a "flippant, pallid, polite beau, who devotes the morning to his toilet, reads a few pages of Chesterfield's letters, and then minces out, to put the infamous principles in practice upon every woman he meets" (I, i). Billy's foil is Colonel Manly, Charlotte's sentimental soldier brother, who, Charlotte admits, is the "very counterpart and reverse" of herself, and who would ride "an hundred miles to relieve a distressed object, or to do a gallant act in the service of his country" (II, i).

The servants too are contrasted. Dimple's man Jessamy is a carbon copy of his master—a pretentious, Chesterfield-quoting fop—but Manly's "waiter" is the simple Jonathan, a farm boy who styles himself a "true born Yankee American son of liberty" (III, i) and has no knowledge of fashion, courtship, or city life.

Tyler's plot structuring also serves to emphasize the difference between American plain dealing and European affectation. Each of the comedy's five acts is composed of two scenes of sharp contrast. The opening scene shows Charlotte gossiping and discussing fashions and beaux with her friend Letitia; the next scene gives us Maria, singing a sentimental song and soliloquizing on the virtue of filial piety. In the first scene of the second act, Charlotte and Letitia meet Manly, who has just arrived in town, and dramatic tension is achieved in the contrast between the ladies' flippancy and the Colonel's sobriety. This contrast is paralleled in the next scene when Jonathan encounters Jessamy, effecting on the servants' level the same distinction just seen among the gentry. By using such alternation and parallelism throughout, Tyler achieved dramatic interest and embodied his "contrast" theme in character and action, with a minimum of moralizing or preaching.

There is little overt action in the first half of *The Contrast*. The play's first three acts are devoted mainly to establishing the characters and the central situation, which is a love intrigue. Billy Dimple is betrothed to the sentimental Maria because of an agreement made between the boy's late father and his friend old Van Rough, Maria's father. Dimple does not love Maria, however, and makes himself disagreeable to her in order to court freely both Charlotte and Letitia—the former for her beauty, the latter for her fortune. Thus, Billy juggles three amours simultaneously and tries to keep each lady from discovering what a deceptive cad he really is.

A subplot with the servants reinforces the courtship theme. Jessamy, appalled at Jonathan's lack of sophistication, schools him in the gentlemanly art of making love and sets him upon Jenny, Van Rough's maid, so that he may practice his technique on her. Jenny finds Jonathan's naiveté ridiculous and when the Yankee tries to kiss her she boxes his ears. Jonathan learns that city ways are not for him.

It is in the fourth act that the plot begins to move. We learn that Colonel Manly, mistaking Van Rough's house for his own lodgings, has entered it and met Maria. Naturally, the two sentimentalists are deeply attracted to each other. When old Van Rough receives a letter informing him that young Dimple is in debt to the tune of seventeen thousand pounds, the old man has second thoughts about giving his daughter to the prodigal Billy. He then overhears a scene of tender sentiment between Maria and Manly in which the two reluctantly agree to part. Manly is, after all, too honorable to court a lady who has been promised to another, and Maria is too sensible of her filial duty to break off with Dimple. Dimple, meanwhile, has planned assignations with both Charlotte and Letitia for the same evening.

In the final scene all these threads of intrigue come together. Manly, hidden in a closet, overhears Dimple force himself upon Charlotte, and comes forward, sword in hand, to challenge the cad. Van Rough arrives in time to part the combatants and to confront Dimple with the evidence of his indebtedness. When Dimple attempts to minimize his guilt, Letitia, who has hidden behind a screen and overheard Dimple's addresses to Charlotte, comes forward and exposes the fop for the two-timer that he is. Dimple exits in disgrace, Van Rough consents to the union of Maria and Manly, Charlotte is sincerely contrite for encouraging Dimple's addresses, and Manly closes the comedy with an observation on the play's message: ". . . that probity, virtue, honour, though they should not have received the polish of Europe, will secure to an honest American the good graces of his fair countrywoman, and, I hope, the applause of THE PUBLIC."

The Contrast's debt to eighteenth-century English comedy in general, and to Sheridan's *The School for Scandal* in particular, is obvious. The play's principal concerns are love intrigues, fashion, and social affectation—all handled in a gently satiric mode. The "screen scene" of *The Contrast*'s final moments suggests Sheridan's play, as does the comedy's opening scene, with Charlotte and Letitia discussing the latest fashion in hoopskirts and the town's beaux. They gossip over their friends' affairs and search for potential scandal in all they discuss. "Scandal," Charlotte later tells Letitia, "is but amusing ourselves with the faults, foibles, follies and reputations of our friends" (II, i). Their gossip is worthy of Lady Sneerwell and her infamous crew.

The playhouse was at the center of English society and, as such, was frequently referred to in the comedies of Sheridan and his contemporaries. Tyler suggests that playgoing was a prominent pastime among fashionable New Yorkers of the 1780s as well. The four major references made to playgoing in *The Contrast* give us some insight into the theatrical milieu of Tyler's time. In a scene with Jonathan, Jessamy tells how his master Dimple "employs his leisure-hours in marking out the plays," with notations for audience laughter:

. . . that the ignorant may know where to laugh; and that pit, box, and gallery may keep time together, and not have a snigger in one part of the house, a broad grin in the other, and a d——d grum look in the third. How delightful to see the audience all smile together, then look on their books, then twist their mouths into an agreeable simper, then altogether shake the house with a general ha, ha, ha! loud as a full chorus of Handel's, at an Abbey-commemoration.

(V, i)

Dimple himself tells of seeing a play on the previous evening and finding it so tedious that "I sat with my back to the stage all the time, admiring a much better actress than any there; —a lady who played the fine woman to perfection" (IV, i). Dimple, of course, detests anything homegrown and finds little to admire in American actors. He describes as "torture" his going to see the "miserable mummers, whom you call actors, murder comedy, and make a farce of tragedy." Tyler's satiric touch here is the more delightful when one realizes that the actors of *The Contrast* were themselves the "miserable mummers" Dimple deplores—the members of the Old American Company.

In yet another reference to the theater, Charlotte gives her brother Manly a long description of an evening's party at the playhouse, an account that we may accept as an accurate portrait of Tyler's audience:

There is Billy Simper, Jack Chassé, and Colonel Van Titter, Miss Promonade, and the two Miss Tambours, sometimes make a party, with some other ladies, in a side-box at the play. Everything is conducted with such decorum, —first we bow round to the company in general, then to each one in particular, then we have so many inquiries after each other's health, and we are so happy to meet each other, and it is so many ages since we last had that pleasure. . . . Then the curtain rises, then our sensibility is all awake, and then by the mere force of apprehension, we torture some harmless expression into a double meaning, which the poor author never dreamt of, and then we have recourse to our fans, and then we blush, and then the gentlemen jog one another, peep under the fan, and make the prettiest remarks; and then we giggle and they simper, and they giggle and we simper, and then the curtain drops, and then for nuts and oranges, and then we bow, and it's pray Ma'am take it, and pray Sir keep it, and oh! not for the world, Sir: and then the curtain rises again, and then we blush, and giggle, and simper, and bow, all over again. Oh! the sentimental charms of a side-box conversation!

(II, ii)

The most extended reference to playgoing in *The Contrast* is Jonathan's account of having seen "The School for Scandalization" (III, i). It is a comic highlight of the play, and the fun derives from Jonathan's total ignorance of having been at the theater and seen a play. He would never knowingly attend the theater, for he firmly believes the playhouse to be the "devil's drawing-room" and the "shop where the devil hangs out the vanities of the world, upon the tenterhooks of temptation." He had come upon the playhouse while searching for "one Mr. Morrison, the *hocus pocus* man" (juggler) and was shown "away clean up to the garret, just like a meeting-house gallery." His description of audience behavior is somewhat different from Charlotte's:

> And so I saw a power of topping folks, all sitting round in little cabbins, just like father's corn-cribs; —and then there was such a squeaking with the fiddles, and such a tarnal blaze with the lights, my head was near turned. At last the people that sat near me set up such a hissing— hiss— like so many mad cats; and then they went thump, thump, thump . . . and stampt away, just like the nation.

When the play had finally begun, Jonathan still had been unaware that he was in a theater: "They lifted up a great green cloth, and let us look right into the next neighbour's house." He then describes the "family" he watched, which included a "poor, good natured, curse of a husband, and a sad rantipole of a wife" (Sir Peter and Lady Teazle of Sheridan's comedy), as well as one "Mr. Joseph," who "talked as sober and as pious as a minister" (Sheridan's Joseph Surface). Jonathan's favorite member of the "family," however, was a character whose description provided Tyler with *The Contrast*'s best theater joke:

> I liked one little fellow. . . . He had red hair, and a little round plump face like mine, only not altogether so handsome. His name was Darby: —that was his baptizing name, his other name I forgot. Oh! it was, Wig— Wag— Wag-all, Darby Wag-all. . . . He is a cute fellow.

The actor who played Jonathan was the leading comedian of the Old American Company, Thomas Wignell, who also had played Darby in John O'Keeffe's *The Poor Soldier*, performed on the same bill with *The Contrast*. The audience must have enjoyed immensely Wignell's description of himself and his reference to his performance as Darby, as well as his praise of himself as a "cute fellow."

Jonathan is Tyler's finest character creation, and one that distinguishes *The Contrast* from typical English comedy. Jonathan gives the comedy its distinctly American flavor. The play's other characters are essentially recreations of familiar character types from the English comedy of manners, but the Yankee Jonathan is an original. The real-life Yankee of Tyler's time was an intensely patriotic, goodhearted, but naive New England rustic who had no use for aristocratic pretensions. Tyler drew upon these qualities in creating Jonathan, the prototype for scores of Yankee comic characters in subsequent American plays.

Jonathan's speech is peppered with homely words and phrases that set him apart from the more sophisticated characters: "what the dogs," "by the living jingo," "dang it all," "tarnation," and so on. He is all the more the Yankee for being contrasted to Jessamy, with whom he appears almost exclusively. Jessamy asks the Yankee if he is Manly's servant, and Jonathan replies indignantly that he is the Colonel's "waiter" and a "true blue son of liberty." He puts Jessamy in his place with: "No man shall master me: my father has as good a farm as the colonel." He can't quite cope with Jessamy's fine language, rendering "insurgents" as "sturgeons," "gallantry" as "girl huntry," and "poignancy" as "pugnancy." He doesn't know the meaning of "kiss," for he has always called it "buss."

Jessamy convinces the Yankee that he should undertake the courtship of Jenny, the maid, and when Jonathan leaves, Jessamy triumphantly declares: "Now will this blundering dog sicken Jenny with his nauseous pawings, until she flies into my arms for very ease. How sweet will the contrast be, between the blundering Jonathan, and the courtly and accomplished Jessamy!" (II, ii). This is Tyler at his ironic best. The "contrast" is indeed "sweet," but our sympathy is all with the crude but genuine Jonathan, not with the affected and foppish Jessamy.

Jonathan's scenes provide the comic highlights in *The Contrast* and illustrate most effectively Tyler's theme: the superiority of native American simplicity over the complex and artificial social codes of European culture. In this respect *The Contrast* is most definitely a product of the Revolutionary spirit and a testimony to patriotic fervor. It is also an eminently stageworthy comedy—one that is more effective on the stage than on the page.

The Contrast even today receives periodic stagings. It was produced in New York in a musical version in November of 1972, and a number of educational theaters included it in their seasons for the American Bicentennial in 1976. Anyone who has seen *The Contrast* acted with intelligence and style can attest to its durability and charm. America's first comedy was a product of which its citizenry could well be proud.

3. WILLIAM DUNLAP: "FATHER OF THE AMERICAN DRAMA"

Playwright, critic, historian, novelist, biographer, painter, theatrical manager—William Dunlap was one of the foremost figures in the cultural life of the new American nation. As the country's first professional dramatist, he gave to the stage nearly sixty plays, including adaptations and translations, as well as originals. Whereas American dramatists before him had engaged in playwriting only as an avocation, Dunlap managed to combine writing with his managerial career and thus become the first American (apart from actors) to make his living largely from the theater.

Dunlap was born in Perth Amboy, New Jersey, on February 11, 1766, the only son of Samuel Dunlap, a shopkeeper. His early interest in creative work led him to painting, a curious choice for a youth who had lost the sight in his right eye at the age of twelve (the result of an accident with a piece of firewood). At the age of seventeen, Dunlap was presented with the opportunity to paint a portrait of General George Washington, and his admiration for the nation's first president was to become evident later in some of his plays. Washington appears, for example, as a character in Dunlap's major play, *André*.

In pursuit of his interest in painting, Dunlap traveled to London in 1784 to study with Benjamin West; it was there that he succumbed to the magic of the theater. In London Dunlap was able to see several of Shakespeare's plays, as well as more recent successes such as Sheridan's *The School for Scandal* and *The Critic*. His interest in painting soon gave way to a fascination with the theater; he neglected his studies with West; and in 1787 his father called him home from his one and only foreign adventure.

Once again in America, Dunlap immediately launched his career as a dramatist by writing a comedy, *The Modest Soldier*, and submitting it to the Old American Company, headed by John Henry. Henry accepted the play but showed no eagerness to produce it; presumably *The Modest Soldier* failed to provide him with a good acting part. The play was never printed but, from Dunlap's own account of it, it was strongly influenced by Royall Tyler's *The Contrast* and drew upon some of the same comic character types.

Dunlap quickly learned the practical lesson that a successful dramatist must write for his actors, and his next play, *The Father; or, American Shandyism*, was immediately produced by Henry, who found in it a role that would show him off to good advantage. *The Father* was acted in 1789 at New York's John Street Theatre, becoming the second comedy by a native American to be produced professionally (the first being *The Contrast*) and the first such comedy to be printed (also in 1789). It was a considerable success with its audiences and was played seven times, establishing Dunlap as a promising new American dramatist.

The promise was to be swiftly fulfilled, as Dunlap continued turning out new plays for the American Company. In the same year as *The Father*, he wrote a farcical interlude called *Darby's Return*, around which an interesting anecdote concerning George Washington has been preserved.

Dunlap's inspiration for Darby was the title character in John O'Keeffe's *The Poor Soldier* (1783), and the role was played by Thomas Wignell, America's leading low comedian, who had been the original Jonathan of *The Contrast*. At one point in the play Darby, who is recounting his American travels, begins a description of the nation's first president. Washington was among the first-nighters and was said to have looked embarrassed at hearing himself eulogized. The joke came, however, when Darby confesses that the "man in regimentals fine" whom he had just described was "not the one"—that he had not seen Washington at all. At this joke Washington was said to have laughed heartily.

Dunlap became manager of the John Street Theatre from 1796 to 1798, investing in a one-fourth share of the Old American Company with the actors John Hodgkinson and Lewis Hallam. As manager, Dunlap was responsible for the choice of plays, and he contributed several of his own originals and adaptations to the John Street repertory.

Early in 1798 the company moved to the new Park Theatre in New York, and in April of that year Hodgkinson withdrew from the ownership, leaving Dunlap as sole manager. His management was plagued with difficulties: undependable actors, repeated outbreaks of yellow fever and, most importantly, financial problems. In February of 1805 Dunlap, bankrupt, closed the theater and returned to painting.

In his seven-year management of the Park, Dunlap had given the theater thirteen original plays and twenty-four translations—a staggering output for a man also struggling with the problems of management. Unfortunately, many of Dunlap's plays—both the originals and the translations—have been lost. Those that survive indicate that, even in the case of the originals, Dunlap was inclined to borrow ideas for plots and characters extensively from other writers. Of the extant originals, by far the best is *André* (1798), generally regarded as Dunlap's finest play. (*André* is further discussed below.)

As a translator of foreign plays, Dunlap did much to bring the contemporary continental drama to America. His penchant for translations arose, no doubt, from expediency—the need to provide variety and novelty for the audiences of the Park Theatre. All but three of his twenty-seven translations were written during his management of the Park. Thirteen of them are of plays by August Friedrich von Kotzebue (1761–1819), the most popular playwright in the world at that time, often referred to as the "German Shakespeare." Only five of these survive.

The most successful of Dunlap's Kotzebue translations was his first: *The Stranger*, from *Menschenhass und Reue* (1789). *The Stranger*, an extremely sentimental domestic melodrama, appealed greatly to the Park's audience, and its success helped Dunlap to keep the theater open, according to his own account. Unfortunately, the play was never printed.

When Dunlap closed the Park Theatre in 1805, he resumed his interest in painting and focused his attention on nontheatrical endeavors, although he did serve as assistant to Thomas Abthorpe Cooper in the management of the Park from 1806 to 1812. This one theatrical affiliation notwithstanding, Dunlap concentrated, after 1805, on artistic and nondramatic literary pursuits. He published a biography of George Frederick Cooke, one of the nation's major early actors, in 1813 and the historically important *Life of Charles Brockden Brown* two years later.

William Dunlap's career as a dramatist was rekindled briefly in 1827 when the management of the Bowery Theatre commissioned him to provide plays for its audiences. At least three of his works are known to have been produced at the Bowery, the most notable of which is *A Trip to Niagara; or, Travellers in America* (acted 1828, published 1830; *A Trip to Niagara* is further discussed below.)

The writings of Dunlap's final years were all non-dramatic. Most significant among them is his *History of the American Theatre* (1832), a primary source of information on Dunlap himself and his career as dramatist and manager. William Dunlap died on September 28, 1839, and was buried in Perth Amboy.

Dunlap's skill as a dramatist is difficult to assess in detail, since so many of his plays have not survived. Theatrical records show, however, that he enjoyed considerable success in appealing to the tastes of his time, however undiscriminating those tastes may have been. All of his surviving plays, both the comedies and the more serious melodramas and tragedies, are high in exaggerated sentiment and patriotic fervor—a winning combination in post-Revolutionary America.

Dunlap's more general contribution to American theater is easier to assess. As a theatrical manager he exhibited a keen sense of both artistic and moral responsibility, always affirming the ethical and political ideals of the new nation in his own plays and in his choice of those by other dramatists. He did much to encourage the writing of native American plays. Through his adaptations and translations he introduced to American audiences the contemporary French and German dramas as well as the Gothic melodrama.

As historian and critic, Dunlap preserved for us the early records of the American theater, seen from his uniquely personal perspective. And he set critical standards. He put his colleagues on notice that the

American nation deserved, and could produce, a first-rate theatrical tradition, independent of the European heritage from which it derived. William Dunlap was truly the Father of the American Drama.

André

André, Dunlap's best play, is America's first tragedy on a native theme. It was performed under Dunlap's management at the Park Theatre on March 30, 1798, and printed in that same year. The play was not successful with its original audiences, who felt, perhaps, too close to the unfortunate event with which it dealt. Dunlap himself acknowledged that he had waited for a number of years to present the play, hoping to gain some historical perspective.

The drama is based upon the hanging of Major John André, a British agent, in October of 1780. André had collaborated with Benedict Arnold in a plot to surrender West Point to the British commander Sir Henry Clinton. Dunlap's dramatization questions the morality of André's execution, and it may have been the author's sympathetic portrayal of the British spy that caused his audience to receive the piece coolly. André, his treachery notwithstanding, is established throughout the play as a noble and brave soldier.

The tragedy is almost classical in its structural unity. The action passes within a ten-hour period, in and around the village of Tappan and its American encampment. The business of André's treachery, capture, and sentencing have taken place before the play begins. The entire action is focused on André's fate and the futile attempt by Bland, an American captain, to save him.

The first act presents the attitudes of Bland and the other characters toward André's death sentence;

André himself does not appear. Bland is shocked to learn that the condemned man, Arnold's coconspirator, is André, the British officer who once not only saved his life but also nursed him back to health and returned him to the American forces. Bland decides to visit André in his cell.

The second scene of the act shows us M'Donald, an American officer of Scottish descent, in conversation with the General (obviously Washington, although his name is never used). The General is given some fairly sentimental speeches extolling patriotism, liberty, and the American spirit:

> O Patriotism!
> Thou wondrous principle of godlike action.
> Wherever liberty is found, there reigns
> The love of country.
> . . . .
> 'Tis this alone which saves thee, O my country!
> And, till that spirit flies these western shores,
> No power on earth shall crush thee.

M'Donald is seen to be a forceful military man who upholds the rule of law and is short on compassion. When Seward, the General's staff officer, suggests a charitable attitude toward André, who, he feels, is the victim of "fickle Fortune," M'Donald is without charity and declares that André is "sunk by misdeed, not fortune":

> Fortune and chance, O, most convenient words!
> Man runs the wild career of blind ambition,
> Plunges in vice, takes falsehood for his buoy,
> And when he feels the waves of ruin o'er him,
> Curses, "in good set terms," poor Lady Fortune.

The General proves to be the moderating voice in this clash between the compassionate Seward and the unfeeling M'Donald.

In Act II we meet André, who is soliloquizing on his

imminent death and thanking "Kind Heaven" that at least he will leave no grieving widow or lamenting child. He is grateful now that he never married his Honora, whom he still loves but who, he believes, has married another. Bland enters and, in an emotional scene, tries to convince André that his treason is forgivable and that he deserves to live. André, however, seems more sensible of his crime than his defender and asks only that Bland petition the General to commute the sentence from the gallows (a disgrace) to the firing squad. Bland exits to plead with the General.

A second scene is given to another Seward–M'Donald dialogue, this one regarding the new American nation's relationship to her European forebears. Seward advocates total isolationism:

> O, would to heaven
> That in midway between these sever'd worlds
> Rose barriers, all impassable to man,
> Cutting off intercourse, till either side
> Had lost all memory of the other!
> . . . .
> Then might, perhaps, one land on earth be found,
> Free from th' extremes of poverty and riches;
> Where ne'er a scepter'd tyrant should be known,
> Or tyrant lordling, curses of creation.

M'Donald, on the other hand, sees some benefit to be derived from continued intercourse with the European nations:

> Prophet of ill,
> From Europe shall enriching commerce flow,
> And many an ill attendant; but from thence
> Shall likewise flow blest science. Europe's
>   knowledge,
> By sharp experience bought, we should
>   appropriate.

It was a timely debate for Dunlap's audience and one, perhaps, not altogether irrelevant today.

A brief third scene introduces Bland's mother and her two younger children. She learns from a letter that her husband, in British custody, is to be executed in retaliation for the death of André. Accordingly, she rushes out to "save the father of my children."

In the first scene of the third act, Bland makes a most passionate appeal to the General for André's life. The General remains adamant, however, and the emotional Bland loses control completely, ripping the cockade from his hat in defiance of military authority and in repudiation of his duty. (This scene earned hisses from the first-night audience, who saw Bland's act as an unpardonable affront to the Federalist cause. Dunlap was forced to modify the effect of the scene for subsequent performances, adding some fifth-act lines for Bland in which he takes up the cockade once more and apologizes for his behavior.)

Also in the third act, Mrs. Bland tells her son in a tearful scene of bathos that his father's life will be forfeited if Major André dies, thus adding to Bland's determination to save the man. A confrontation between the General and a British Officer concludes with the General's renewed determination to go through with the execution—particularly when a message from the elder Bland arrives entreating the General to "do *your* duty" and disregard his (Bland's) fate. André, learning from Bland that his father is to be killed by the British in retaliation, determines to send a letter to his commander, pleading for the elder Bland's life. This confirms for us André's utter nobility of spirit.

Act IV opens with a violent confrontation between the desperate Bland and the obdurate M'Donald, in which Bland, utterly irrational, tries to provoke M'Donald into a duel. This "reason-versus-passion" encounter ends with Bland rushing off to proclaim M'Donald a coward. The scene shifts to the prison and we meet André's onetime sweetheart, Honora, who declares her continuing love for the condemned man, claiming that her father had spread the false rumor of her marriage to another. (The historical André had a sweetheart named Honora Seward, but she died before André's disgrace. The entire Honora complication plays no part in the movement of the plot and serves only to introduce a note of romantic sentimentality.)

In the final act Bland and M'Donald are reconciled (the scene that was added after the first performance); Bland and André have a tearful farewell scene; news of the release of the elder Bland arrives; and André is shown marching to his execution. A cannon signals his death and Bland voices a final note of sympathy for the British officer:

> O! let my countrymen,
> Henceforward when the cruelties of war
> Arise in their remembrance; when their ready
> Speech would pour forth torrents in their foe's
>   dispraise,
> Think on this act accurst, and lock complaint
>   in silence.
>
> (V, v)

But M'Donald finds a more profound lesson in André's death—one from which all Americans can profit:

> O, may the children of Columbia still
> Be taught by every teacher of mankind,
> Each circumstance of calculative gain,
> Or wounded pride, which prompted our
>   oppressors;
> May every child be taught to lisp the tale;
> And may, in times to come, no foreign force,
> No European influence, tempt to misstate,
> Or awe the tongue of eloquence to silence,
> Still may our children's children deep abhor
> The motives, doubly deep detest the actors;
> Ever remembering that the race who plann'd,
> Who acquiesced, or did the deeds abhor'd,

Has pass'd from off the earth; and, in its stead,
Stand men who challenge love or detestation
But from their proper, individual deeds.
Never let memory of the sire's offence
Descend upon the son.

(V, v)

André has, for a play of its period, much to commend it. Dunlap's handling of blank verse is skillful and, occasionally, genuinely moving. The necessary ingredient of sentiment is present, of course, but not nearly so obtrusively as in most of his other plays. The plot is carefully structured and almost free of artificial contrivance, the sudden appearance of Honora being the major exception.

Dunlap effectively used characterization in *André* to represent varying attitudes toward the central situation. Bland, although passionate, is humane in his fight to save his friend. For him, political matters are secondary to such values as friendship and forgiveness. M'Donald, on the other hand, represents the stern legalistic viewpoint. André's guilt is never at question in the play.

Much of the play's patriotic sentiment, perfectly appropriate to a 1798 American drama, is honestly expressed and can be affecting even for a reader today. Although *André* has not been produced in modern times, it is worthy of staging. A contemporary production, played with sincerity and unabashed patriotism, might provide an enlightening glimpse of America's theatrical heritage as well as a worthwhile entertainment.

A Trip to Niagara; or, Travellers in America

Dunlap's last original play, a slim piece by literary standards, must nevertheless have made an impressive theatrical spectacle, for it enjoyed the longest run of all his plays. It opened at the Bowery Theatre on November 28, 1828, and played almost every night through January 14, 1829. Additionally, it was revived at least twice during the following year.

The success of *A Trip to Niagara* was undoubtedly due to its capitalizing on the current fancy for panoramic scenery and "dioramas." The diorama was a moving strip of painted canvas that unrolled from one spool to another across the back of the stage, creating the illusion that objects and persons in the foreground were in motion. The Bowery's scenery for this Dunlap comedy utilized twenty-five thousand square feet of painted canvas in depicting the moving scenes for a boat trip from New York harbor, up the Hudson to the Erie Canal, and thence to Niagara Falls. In his preface to the comedy, Dunlap admitted with chagrin that the management of the theater considered his play, which he termed a "Farce," as a kind of "running accompaniment to the more important product of the Scene-painter."

The "Trip" of the title is taken by two English visitors to America, Mr. Wentworth and his sister Amelia. They are accompanied by their servants; by John Bull, a fellow Englishman; and by an Irishman, Dennis Dougherty. Wentworth detests America and loses no opportunity to denounce the new nation and its people. Amelia, on the other hand, expresses a sincere appreciation for the natural beauty of the land and the plain-dealing honesty of its inhabitants. Bull, who wishes to marry Amelia, gains from her the promise that if he can cure her brother of his anti-American sentiments, she will be his wife. Bull's attempt to convert Wentworth is the slender thread of plot that serves as an excuse for the play's main attraction, the scenic spectacle.

A Trip to Niagara is written in three acts, and each

act is divided into component scenes, thus providing ample opportunities for scene changes. The play opens in the Wentworth apartment in New York's City Hotel. A second first-act scene is set at *"Steam-boat wharf, bottom of Courtlandt-street, New-York. Bell ringing. The usual bustle. Steam-boat runners inviting passengers. View of Jersey City. Ships in the stream, etc."*

The text of the second act is extremely brief, for it is here that the diorama comes into play. Dunlap specified in his stage directions eighteen separate but continuous scenes, beginning with *"Harbour of New-York. Governor's Island. Ships at anchor,"* and ending with *"Catskill landing."* There is no dialogue during this scenic display; the effect must have been similar to that of a motion picture travelogue.

The third act is composed of six separate scenes, all of which are described in the text in some detail. The audience is shown the *"Mountain, or Pine Orchard House,"* a *"waterfall and cave,"* *"State-street, Albany [with] the Capitol at a distance,"* the *"little falls of the Mohawk,"* the *"Hotel at Buffalo,"* and finally the *"Falls of Niagara"*—in which spectacular setting the comedy closes. It is not surprising that Dunlap attributed the success of his play to the "product of the Scene-painter."

Nevertheless, the text of the play is not without interest. The comedy is notable for including four of the best-known ethnic stereotypes on the stage at the time: the Frenchman, the Yankee, the Irishman, and the Negro.

The first two types are impersonated by Bull in his campaign against Wentworth's prejudices. Bull first appears as the Frenchman, Monsieur Tonson, and behaves so offensively that he serves as a parody of Wentworth himself in his haughty and demanding manner. Wentworth begins to see just how obnoxious a foreign visitor can be, but he has yet to see himself in the portrait. Bull's second impersonation is of the Yankee, Jonathan, modeled after the Jonathan of Tyler's *The Contrast* and one of a long line of such stage stereotypes. It is as Jonathan that Bull effects his conversion of Wentworth. By pretending to speak against his countrymen, Jonathan forces Wentworth, strangely enough, to come to their defense. The entire business of Wentworth's conversion is artificially contrived and is, even for farce, the weakest feature of the plot.

The most interesting of the ethnic types is that of the Negro, Job Jerryson, a waiter in the City Hotel. This character represents the first attempt on the American stage to portray a realistic, educated, free Negro who is intelligent and articulate. Jerryson sees in himself the nobility of Othello; he states that he belongs to an amateur theatrical troupe, the Shakespeare Club. He refuses to call any man "master" and behaves with dignity and restraint. The portrait of Job Jerryson is consistent with Dunlap's well-known animosity toward the institution of slavery and his respect for the free Negro.

Yet another notable character appears in the last act: Leather-Stocking, dressed *"as described in J. F. Cooper's Pioneers."* Leather-Stocking plays no role in the Wentworth–Bull plot, except insofar as he serves to illustrate the romance of the pioneering American and to elaborate upon the natural wonders of the American frontier. Dunlap and Cooper were friends, and the inclusion of Cooper's legendary hero in this comedy is possibly Dunlap's acknowledgment of his friend's contribution to the literature and culture of the new nation.

A Trip to Niagara is more a theatrical entertainment than a drama in the conventional literary sense. Nevertheless, it is entertaining even in the reading. Its low-comedy scenes are genuinely amusing and could well succeed on the stage in the hands of skilled comedians. Its characters (properly, caricatures) are strongly individualized. Amelia particularly emerges as a realistic, independent woman—one of Dunlap's finest female characters. The play is fiercely chauvinistic, but never at the expense of the foreign visitors. (It is, after all, another Englishman who reforms Wentworth.) Finally, *A Trip to Niagara* is one of the least sentimental of all Dunlap's plays, which accounts in part for its genuine humor and its theatrical viability.

4. DUNLAP'S CONTEMPORARIES

Although the figure of William Dunlap dominated the American theatrical scene in the early years of the nineteenth century, he was by no means the only dramatist making meaningful contributions to the American theater. The first three decades of the century produced scores of playwrights, all amateurs of varying accomplishment, whose works received professional productions.

Susanna Haswell Rowson (1762–1824), like Mercy Warren and others, upheld the tradition of the female playwright, writing plays with national themes and strong female characters. Unfortunately, only a single play of hers survives.

John Murdock (1748–1834) and Charles Jared Ingersoll (1782–1862) were two Philadelphians who gave that city a number of plays. Murdock concentrated on the comedy of manners in the vein of Tyler's *The Contrast*, while Ingersoll essayed classical tragedy in blank verse.

In the South, too, the theater offered a challenge to devotees of the dramatic art. John Blake White (1781–1859) and Isaac Hardy (1788–1828) both made important contributions to the Charleston theater. White wrote five plays, three of which were produced there, and a like number of Hardy's works were acted.

One could easily name other dramatists deserving of study, if space allowed: Joseph Hutton (1787–1828), an actor in Philadelphia and New Orleans who wrote five plays, remarkable for their diversity; Samuel Woodworth (1785–1842), whose *The Forest Rose* (1825) was enormously successful, and notable for its Yankee character of Jonathan Ploughboy; John Augustus Stone (1800–1834), whose *Metamora* (1829) was one of the great successes of its age; Samuel B. H. Judah (ca. 1799–1876), a skillful writer of melodramas; Richard Penn Smith (1799–1854), who had at least fifteen of his twenty plays acted; and many more.

There were, however, three dramatists whose contributions to the American theater in the Dunlap era were especially noteworthy: John Daly Burk, Mordecai Manuel Noah, and James Nelson Barker. The plays of these three men represent some of the best work by American writers to be seen on American stages in the first third of the nineteenth century. Several of their plays are well worth the attention of the modern reader.

John Daly Burk (1776?–1808)

Patriotism was perhaps the single dominant theme in early American drama, and the patriotic history play seldom failed to draw an appreciative audience. A major contributor to the genre was John Daly Burk, whose drama of *Bunker-Hill* became one of the more successful patriotic plays of the early nineteenth century.

Burk was not a native American; he was born in Ireland and spent his youth there. He seems to have been a contentious character, frequently involved in controversy. He was expelled from Dublin's Trinity College for his unorthodox political and religious views and was forced literally to flee for his life, dressed in women's clothing and hotly pursued by the British authorities. It was this flight that brought him to Boston in 1796, where he worked as a journalist and editor. He soon moved to New York, pursuing his journalistic career, but was arrested there for having published allegedly libelous and seditious material. Thereafter, Burk lived in Virginia, where he continued to practice law and dabble in literature, as well as act in an amateur theater group there.

Unfortunately, Burk's temperamental nature and outspoken political views brought him to an untimely end. In a tavern conversation one evening he began haranguing against Napoleonic France and called the French a "pack of rascals." He was promptly challenged to a duel by one Monsieur Coquebert, who, on April 10, 1808, put a bullet through his heart.

As many as seven plays have been attributed to Burk, but only three have been proven his with complete certainty: *Bunker-Hill; or, The Death of General Warren* (1797); *Female Patriotism; or, The Death of Joan d'Arc* (1798); and *Bethlem Gabor, Lord of Transylvania* (1807). The last is a Gothic revenge melodrama with a happy ending, notable only for the fact that Burk himself played the title role in its Richmond premiere. *Bunker-Hill* and *Female Patriotism* are the two of Burk's plays that merit attention by the modern reader.

Female Patriotism is not so well known as *Bunker-Hill*, but it is the superior play from a literary standpoint. Arthur Hobson Quinn called it "one of the bright spots that reward the reader of our early drama,"[1] and a more recent critic has judged it "one of the best American plays written in the eighteenth century."[2] It was staged at New York's Park Theatre, on April 13, 1798, but was poorly received and slipped quietly into relative obscurity vis-à-vis the more spectacular *Bunker-Hill*.

The play's chief attraction is the characterization of Joan of Arc, who is drawn as a realistic and sympathetic woman. Her persuasive power, which leads of course to her death, is focused not so much upon religious ideals as it is toward political ends. She works to achieve republican status for her native France. Even in historical drama, Burk's republicanism and devotion to the American cause are evident.

Compared to *Female Patriotism, Bunker-Hill* might strike the modern reader as so much maudlin and sentimental claptrap, but it enjoyed amazing popularity and held the stage for years, appearing regularly as a Fourth of July attraction. It was first staged at Boston's Haymarket Theatre on February 17, 1797. Its success was all the more amazing for the fact that its critical notices were almost all negative. William Dunlap called it a "deplorable play" and a rival theater manager dubbed it the "most execrable of the Grub Street kind" of presentation. Nevertheless, its fervent patriotism and spectacular staging saw it through a remarkable ten performances in its initial run, as well as several printings. Burk made two thousand dollars on it, an almost unheard-of sum for a single play.

Burk called *Bunker-Hill* "an Historic Tragedy"; its subject matter is, of course, the storming of Bunker Hill by the British in 1775. The play is written in five acts and twelve scenes, although it is fairly short. Its dialogue is in blank verse that rarely rises to the level of true poetry. The plot focuses on two separate intrigues, related only by the impending battle itself.

The play's central figure is the American General Warren, although he is given little to do but expound upon the glories of the American cause and vilify the British. The more dramatic conflict is that of the subplot, a love intrigue between Abercrombie, a British soldier, and Elvira, daughter of a wealthy Carolinian. Abercrombie is placed in the conventional "love-versus-honor" dilemma, having to choose whether to fight with the English at Bunker Hill and risk loss of his beloved Elvira or to throw down his arms and flee with her, thus becoming a traitor to the British cause. There is much agonizing and shedding of tears over the decision, but Abercrombie finally opts for honor and dies in the storming of the hill, after which Elvira runs mad. She appears, Ophelia-like, at the battle ground, "*her hair loose; her bosom disordered; her eyes wild and haggard*," and, after an interlude of distracted raving, falls on the corpse of her beloved Abercrombie.

It was certainly Burk's intention to make General Warren appear utterly noble in his love of country, but the officer's dialogue is so excessively chauvinistic as to render him almost a fanatic. Burk had intended to dedicate the printed text of the play to President John Adams, but after Adams had seen the play, he told one of the actors: "My friend, General Warren, was a scholar and a gentleman but your author has made him a bully and a blackguard."[3] Burk therewith dedicated the play to Aaron Burr.

Aside from its effusive patriotism, *Bunker-Hill*'s chief attraction was undoubtedly its spectacular scenic effects. The climactic scene is, of course, the storming of the hill—a scene without dialogue that is said to have lasted fifteen minutes. In a letter to John Hodgkinson, part-manager of the John Street Theatre, Burk described the playing of this scene in Boston. It is a rare document on early American stagecraft, worth noting here in part:

The English marched in two divisions from one extremity of the stage, where they ranged after coming from the wings; when they come to the foot of the hill, the Americans fire—the English fire—six or seven of your men should be taught to fall—the fire should be frequent for some minutes. The English retire to the front of the stage—second time of English advance from the wing near the hill—firing commences—they are again beaten back—windows on the stage should be open to let the smoke out. Again the English make the attack and mount the hill. After a brisk fire the Americans leave works and meet them. Here is room for effect, if the scuffle be nicely managed. Sometimes the English fall back, sometimes the Americans—two or three Englishmen rolling down the hill. . . . When the curtain rises in the fifth [act], the appearance of the whole is good—Charlestown on fire, the breastwork of wood, the Americans appearing over the works and the muzzles of their guns, the English and the American music, the attack of the hill, the falling of the English troops, Warren's half descending the hill, and animating the Americans, the smoke and confusion, altogether produce an effect scarce credible.[4]

In addition to the battle scene, *Bunker-Hill* offers opportunities for other visual treats: a variety of interior and exterior settings; a company of British troops who "*fly across the stage as if pursued*"; the disembarkation of the English forces at the foot of Bunker Hill; and, in the final scene, General Warren's funeral cortege. This procession, described in an extensive stage direction, features the grieving American troops, "*children bearing flowers*," the bier, six standards "*decorated with republican emblems*," and "*two virgins*" (!) who sing "Roslin Castle" over the coffin. Whatever his qualifications as a serious dramatist, John Daly Burk knew how to please an audience.

Mordecai Manuel Noah (1785–1851)

National plays should be encouraged. They have done everything for the British nation, and can do much for us; they keep alive the recollection of important events, by representing them in a manner at once natural and alluring. We have a fine scope, and abundant materials to work with, and a noble country to justify the attempt.

Thus wrote M. M. Noah in the preface to his best-known play, *She Would Be a Soldier*, a fine example of the American patriotic comedy of the early nineteenth century. Noah had no illusions, however, about his own importance as a dramatist. He repeatedly styled himself an "amateur" playwright with "no idea of being the first to descend into the arena, and become a gladiator for the American Drama."[5] His career lay in politics and journalism; playwriting was a diversion.

Noah was born in Philadelphia on July 19, 1785. He became involved in journalism as early as 1800 and eventually edited the Charleston *City Gazette*, provoking considerable hostility from his readers for his political editorials, written under the pseudonym of "Muley Molack." He was widely traveled, interested in literature and the theater and, as his writings attest, possessed of a delightful sense of humor. Secretary of State James Monroe named him Consul to Tunis in 1813, and during the 1820s he served in a number of political posts in New York. He died there on March 22, 1851.

Seven plays have been attributed to M. M. Noah. His first effort was *The Fortress of Sorrento* (1808), a treatment of the Leonora/Fidelio story that was never acted. Next came *Paul and Alexis; or, The Orphans of the Rhine*, which was first acted at Charleston in 1812 and subsequently at London's Covent Garden theater in February of 1814 under the title *The Wandering Boys*, where it enjoyed considerable success, running for eight nights. This melodrama, adapted from a French play by Pixérécourt, was finally played at New York's Park Theatre in 1815 (some accounts give 1820), also under the title *The Wandering Boys*.

Noah's next play was *She Would Be a Soldier* (1819), discussed more fully below. This was followed by *The Siege of Tripoli* (Park Theatre, May 15, 1820), which has not survived, and *Marion; or, The Hero of Lake George* (Park Theatre, November 25, 1821). Then came *The Grecian Captive; or, The Fall of Athens* (Park Theatre, June 17, 1822), regarding which production an amusing account has survived. In a letter to William Dunlap, Noah wrote of the first night of *The Grecian Captive*:

> As a "good house" was of more consequence to the actor than fame to the author, it was resolved that the hero of the piece should make his appearance on an elephant, and the heroine on a camel, which were procured from a neighbouring *menagerie*, and the *tout ensemble* was sufficiently imposing, only it happened that the huge elephant, in shaking his skin, so rocked the castle on his back, that the Grecian general nearly lost his balance, and was in imminent danger of coming down from his "high estate," to the infinite merriment of the audience.[6]

Noah's final play was *The Siege of Yorktown*, acted at the Park on September 8, 1824, during the visit of Lafayette.

She Would Be a Soldier; or, The Plains of Chippewa was Noah's major contribution to American drama. By his own admission, he wrote the play in three days, expressly for the actress Miss Leesugg (later Mrs. Hackett), who played the "breeches part" of the title character. The play is a patriotic comedy based loosely upon the historical battle of Chippewa Plains in July of 1814. It was first performed at the Park Theatre on June 21, 1819, and held the stage for at least thirty years. Edwin Forrest found it sufficiently attractive to enact the Indian Chief in an 1825 production.

The "She" of the title is Christine, a spirited young woman who loves a soldier, Lenox. Christine's father, however, has promised her hand to Jerry, an insensitive bumpkin whom Christine can't abide. Thus, dressed in boy's clothing, she decides to run away and join her beloved Lenox. When she turns up at the American camp, she sees Lenox in the company of another woman, the General's daughter, and mistakenly believes that her lover has broken faith with her. Desolate, she enlists as a soldier so that she can be near Lenox. While on guard duty, she impulsively makes an unauthorized trespass into the General's tent and is arrested. She is tried for treason, pleads guilty, and asks for death. In the climactic final scene she is led, in solemn procession, before the firing squad, but not before having cast away the miniature that Lenox had earlier given her—a miniature that an officer retrieved and, recognizing Lenox's portrait, took to him. The firing squad raise their rifles and are about to fire when Lenox rushes in to save his beloved, revealing her true identity. Meanwhile, the Battle of Chippewa Plains has been fought and won, off stage, and all ends happily.

A subplot involves the British Captain Pendragon, his French valet La Role, and an Indian Chief. Pendragon and La Role, two fops, are made to exchange their fancy European dress for Indian war regalia and fight with the Indians against the American settlers. After losing the battle, all three are brought before the General and, expecting death, receive instead a lecture on patriotism and a full pardon. The General sums up the play's action and message:

All things have terminated happily. Our arms have been triumphant, and our gallant soldiers rewarded with the approbation of their country. Love has intwined a wreath for your brows, Lenox, and domestic peace and happiness await you; and when old age draws on apace, may you remember the PLAINS OF CHIPPEWA, and feel towards Britain as freemen should feel towards all the world: "*Enemies in war—in peace, friends.*"

There is much in *She Would Be a Soldier* to please an American audience of 1819. The sprightly character of Christine is quite appealing, although her several sentimental soliloquies of the "maiden-in-distress" variety may strike the modern reader as excessively emotional. Aside from these soliloquies, however, the play's prose dialogue is quite realistic and often genuinely amusing. Opportunities for visual appeal abound: a variety of settings, peasant dances, military drills and marching, a court martial, and the very thrilling ceremony of Christine's being led before the firing squad.

The characters of the comedy are nicely individualized, although based upon popular stereotypes of the period. The Indian Chief personifies the type of the "noble savage," all courage and eloquent nobility; his final conversion to the American side must have pleased the audience. Pendragon and La Role represent the affected and foolish European gentry, with which no plain-dealing Patriot could have any patience. They are, accordingly, debased and ridiculed while in their Indian garb and war paint. Jerry, the farmboy, continues the tradition of the Yankee plowboy, first made popular in the Jonathan of Tyler's *The Contrast*, although he is too much of a boob to have Jonathan's appeal.

She Would Be a Soldier is by no means a great play, but it serves as a fine example of dramatic comedy pressed into service as an expression of patriotic fervor in America's early years.

James Nelson Barker (1784–1858)

Like Burk and Noah, James Nelson Barker was strictly an amateur dramatist who made his living in nontheatrical pursuits—namely, military and government service. Only half of his ten plays have survived, but three of the remaining five—*The Indian Princess*, *Marmion*, and *Superstition*—are major contributions to early American drama.

Barker was born in Philadelphia on June 17, 1784, the son of General John Barker, mayor of that city in 1808 and 1809. The younger Barker followed in his father's footsteps by becoming Mayor of Philadelphia himself in 1819. Prior to that, however, he had distinguished himself in military pursuits, serving in the War of 1812 as captain in the Second Artillery Regiment and, after the war, as Assistant Adjutant General of the Fourth Military District with the rank of major.

In the years 1829 to 1838 Barker indulged his literary ambitions by writing poetry, serving at the same time as Collector of the Port of Philadelphia, a post to which he was appointed by President Jackson. America's next President, James Van Buren, named him First Comptroller of the Treasury, and he remained principally connected with the Treasury Department until his death on March 9, 1858.

Barker exemplifies the American playwright who was dedicated to American themes. Although he was eclectic in his choice of source material, most of his plays embodied American concerns. He frequently drew upon colonial history, as in *Superstition*, his finest play.

Barker's first acted play was written at the special

request of William Wood, then manager of Philadelphia's Chestnut Street Theatre. *Tears and Smiles*, a contemporary comedy of manners, opened at the Chestnut Street to a "brilliant audience and with complete success," according to its author, on March 4, 1807. The play, like so many comedies of its time, owed much to Tyler's *The Contrast*. Like that play, *Tears and Smiles* has its fashionable lovers, as well as its Europeanized fop—this time Fluttermore, who affects French deportment, a variation on the Anglicized Mr. Dimple of Tyler's comedy.

Barker also continued the Yankee plowboy stereotype in *Tears and Smiles*, imitating Tyler's Jonathan. Barker's Yankee is Nathan Yank, a character he wrote especially for Joseph Jefferson, its original impersonator. "Such a Yankee as I drew!" Barker later wrote. "The truth is, I had never even seen a Yankee at the time."[7] In spite of its initial success, *Tears and Smiles* offers little to amuse a modern reader.

Barker's next surviving play is *The Indian Princess; or, La Belle Sauvage* (Chestnut Street Theatre, April 6, 1808), the first extant American play on the Pocahontas story and the first American Indian play to be produced.[8] *The Indian Princess*, an operatic melodrama with music by John Bray, enjoyed success with audiences and critics alike. The New York *Evening Post* review for June 13 termed it, "in point of dramatic composition, one of the most chaste and elegant plays ever written in the United States."[9] The play was produced at London's Drury Lane Theatre as *Pocahontas; or, The Indian Princess* on December 15, 1820, thus becoming possibly the first native American play to be produced in London after an American premiere.

The Indian Princess represents a definite improvement in Barker's dramatic technique, and it contains at least one scene of genuine merit: the love scene between Pocahontas and Rolfe (III, ii), written in blank verse. Commenting upon Barker's poetry in this scene,

Quinn wrote that the dramatist was "then excelled by none in his native country and by few, if any, of those who were writing at that time for the stage in England."[10] Barker used as his source material John Smith's *General History of Virginia* (1624), and the manner in which he transformed his source—selecting, rearranging, and altering fact—indicates his facility in structuring a dramatic plot rich in action, humor, and romance. He was to display even more skill, however, in his next effort, *Marmion*.

Marmion; or, The Battle of Flodden Field, based upon Sir Walter Scott's poem, was Barker's most successful play. It opened at the Park Theatre in New York on April 13, 1812, and subsequently "ran like wild fire through all our theatres," according to its author.

Barker's own account of a "very innocent fraud upon the public" in connection with *Marmion* makes a significant comment upon the prejudice against native plays with which he and his contemporaries were constantly forced to deal:

> We insinuated that the piece was a London one, had it sent to our theatre from New York, where it was made to arrive in the midst of rehearsal, in the presence of the actors, packed up exactly *like pieces we were in the habit of receiving from London. It was opened with great gravity, and announced without any author being alluded to.* None of the company were in the secret, as I well knew "these actors cannot keep counsel," not even the prompter.[11]

Thus, *Marmion* was first advertised as written by "Thomas Morton, Esq.," and only after its success was assured did Barker admit to its authorship. The play enjoyed successful revivals throughout America as late as 1848.

Marmion attests to Barker's facility in taking historical material—in this case from both Scott's poem and Holinshed's chronicles—and shaping it to reflect contemporary American concerns. At the core of the play is England's brutal treatment of Scotland in the sixteenth century, but the parallel to the English-American situation in 1812 was obvious to Barker's audience.

When *Marmion* premiered, Congress was debating the declaration of war against Great Britain, and resentment against England was at a fever pitch. In the climactic scene of the play (IV, iv), King James of Scotland protests to Marmion, ambassador from Henry VIII, of the wrongs that his country has suffered at the hands of the English. It is a powerful scene of confrontation, which James brings to a close with stirring eloquence:

> . . . I burn to speak it—
> Murder and pillage, England's constant agents,
> Roamed through our land, and harboured in our
>   bays!
> Our peaceful border sacked, our vessels
>   plundered,
> Our abused liegemen robbed, enslaved and
>   slaughtered.
> My lord, my lord, under such injuries,
> How shall a free and gallant nation act?
> Still lay its sovereignty at England's feet—
> Still basely ask a boon from England's bounty—
> Still vainly hope redress from England's justice?
> No! by our martyred fathers' memories,
> The land may sink—but, like a glorious wreck,
> 'Twill keep its colours flying to the last.

At the first Philadelphia performance, six months after war had been declared, this scene won a ten-minute ovation from the cheering audience at the Chestnut Street Theatre.

The fourth extant Barker play, *How to Try a Lover*, has little to do with American themes or concerns, but it is a better comedy than *Tears and Smiles*. Although it was written and printed in 1817, it was not performed until 1836, on March 26 at Philadelphia's Arch Street Theatre. It was acted then under the title of *The Court of Love*. Adapted from a French novel of thirteenth-century Spain, *How to Try a Lover* is a comedy of romantic entanglement, replete with disguise, intrigue, and deception. Its characters are little more than familiar types and its action is trivial, but the play shows considerable skill in its snappy dialogue and tight construction. In this play, Barker proved himself an able dramatic craftsman, shaping the episodic material of a picaresque novel into a unified dramatic action. He was already by this time an accomplished dramatist, although his masterpiece, *Superstition*, was not to appear for another seven years.

Superstition; or, The Fanatic Father was first acted at the Chestnut Street Theatre on March 12, 1824. It was not so well received as *The Indian Princess* or *Marmion*, although it is certainly the finest of Barker's dramatic works. Quinn called it the "best play that had so far been written in America,"[12] and the more recent commentator, W. J. Meserve, has gone so far as to term it the "single outstanding American play written during the first quarter of the nineteenth century."[13]

In shaping his plot for *Superstition* Barker drew upon colonial history of 1675, but again he altered fact in order to create an effective drama. On the title page of the printed text Barker called the play a tragedy, although it is apt to strike the modern reader more as romantic melodrama.

The play's tragic figure and chief attraction is Ravensworth, clergyman of a small colonial village. Ravensworth controls his congregation through fear and intimidation and is fanatical in his obsession with

the power of evil and its destructive effect upon man-
kind. To Ravensworth, life is a constant struggle
against the machinations of Satan:

> We have grown
> Luke-warm in zeal, degenerate in spirit;—
> I would root out with an unsparing hand,
> The weeds that choke the soil;—pride and rank
>   luxury
> Spring up around us;—alien sectaries,
> Spite of the whip and axe, infest our limits;
> Bold infidelity, dark sorcery—
> . . . .
> The powers of darkness are at work among us.
>   (I, i)

The "powers of darkness," Ravensworth believes,
reside in Isabella, a relative newcomer to the village
who has little respect for religion—at least the religion
of Ravensworth's kind. Isabella's background is
shrouded in mystery, which only adds to Ravensworth's suspicion that she is an instrument of the
devil. The antagonism between the two is complicated
by the love affair of the clergyman's daughter, Mary,
with Isabella's son, Charles, a strong-willed youth who
has been expelled from college and is returning home
as the play opens.

Into the village come Sir Reginald and George
Egerton, two Englishmen on a mission from King
Charles II to seek out a fugitive regicide who is implicated in the death of Charles I. Also, a mysterious
figure identified only as "the Unknown" appears and
leads the villagers in repulsing an Indian attack, thus
establishing himself as a powerful and "supernatural
visitant."

Ravensworth eventually succeeds in having Isabella
arrested and brought to trial on charges of witchcraft.
Charles steals into Mary's chamber for a love tryst,
and the two are discovered by Ravensworth, who

vows to try Charles for the attempted rape of his daughter. In the climactic trial scene, Isabella answers Ravensworth's accusation of sorcery with stirring eloquence, causing the minister to back down and shift focus to Charles's supposed crimes. Accused of attempted rape, Charles refuses to defend himself, so that his beloved Mary will not be forced to testify and thus become implicated in their shared passion. As a storm begins to rage outside, Ravensworth's accusative ravings reach a climax, Mary swoons, and Charles is led out to be executed. In the final moments, we learn that "the Unknown" is Isabella's long-lost father and the fugitive regicide sought by the Egertons. Charles is then revealed to have been a son of King Charles II at the very moment that his body is brought back on stage. Mary revives and, seeing the corpse of her beloved, goes mad and dies of a broken heart. The final stage direction focuses on Ravensworth's unspoken grief and remorse as he realizes that his "superstition" has caused the death of his daughter and only joy.

In narrative outline, *Superstition* appears to be quite melodramatic and filled with implausible coincidence, but Barker managed to render the proceedings remarkably convincing and, in places, genuinely moving. Ravensworth's fanatical bigotry is relieved by his moments of paternal concern; he truly cherishes Mary. The blank verse of the dialogue contains passages of some eloquence, as when Isabella answers the accusation of witchcraft. The climactic trial scene with its raging storm is skillfully managed to provide a maximum of theatricality and dramatic intensity.

Superstition antedates Arthur Miller's *The Crucible* by 130 years, but the modern reader cannot miss the similarity of setting and theme. Barker's play exhibits many of the indulgences of the melodramatic style of its time, but it seems strangely modern in its indictment of intolerance, fanaticism, and the "superstition" of religious bigotry.

5. ENTER THE ACTOR-DRAMATIST

Writing for the stage was far from a lucrative occupation in America during the first half of the nineteenth century. Dunlap had managed to make his living from the theater only by combining playwriting with his work as a manager and producer. Even so, he went bankrupt and was forced to abandon the theater for a number of years. His contemporaries—Burk, Noah, Barker, and their fellows—wrote plays strictly as a sideline, making their livings in other pursuits.

As the century progressed, however, the phenomenon of the actor-dramatist evolved, so that by the late nineteenth century many dramatists were combining playwriting with careers on the stage. Two early examples of the American actor-dramatist were John Howard Payne and Anna Cora Mowatt Ritchie. Payne was Dunlap's contemporary and the only American besides Dunlap to make a career of playwriting—in his case, combined with acting rather than managing. Mrs. Mowatt, active a generation later, was an actress first and foremost, but she did pen one of the finest nineteenth-century American comedies, *Fashion*.

Payne and Mowatt represent the beginning of the actor-dramatist tradition that was to culminate in such stellar figures as Dion Boucicault and James A. Herne in the latter half of the century, and their contributions to the American drama were considerable.

John Howard Payne (1791–1852)

No theatrical personality in the first third of the nineteenth century did more to establish the respectability of the American dramatist abroad than did John Howard Payne. Unlike any other of his American colleagues, Payne spent nearly twenty years abroad, earning considerable repute as an actor and playwright in England and France.

Born in New York on June 9, 1791, John Howard was the son of William Payne, headmaster of a Long Island academy. In 1796 the family moved to Boston, where the younger Payne acted in school plays and evidenced a formidable precociousness. In 1805 he returned to New York and immediately established himself as a youthful attraction in the social, literary, and theatrical life of the city.

Payne's first play was produced while he was a mere fourteen years of age. *Julia; or, The Wanderer* was acted at the Park Theatre on February 7, 1806, and was notable for the critical furor that it occasioned. *Julia*, advertised as "written by Eugenius, a gentlemen of New York," is a comedy-melodrama of remarkable sophistication and daring dialogue, considering the callowness of its author. The critics wrote of its "criminal sentiments and indecorous observations," its "indecencies and smutty incidents," and its "stilted and indecent language."[1] Young Master Payne had clearly made his mark on the American theater.

The penning of *Julia* notwithstanding, Payne's initial ambition was to become an actor. He made his professional debut at the age of seventeen as Young Norval in Scottish clergyman-playwright John

Home's *Douglas* at the Park Theatre, February 24, 1809. The "boy actor" was a novelty then much in vogue, and Payne set himself the task of emulating England's Master William Betty. His Norval was a great success and he was quickly hailed as the "American Roscius." The critic of the *American Citizen* called him the "*first* theatrical genius our nation has produced," and another writer subsequently proclaimed him "superior to [Master] Betty" in a number of roles.[2] America had its boy actor.

In the season 1809–10 Payne played at least ten major roles in nine American cities. He was the first native American to play Hamlet. (His Ophelia was Elizabeth Poe, mother of the then-infant Edgar Allan.) Having conquered America, Payne decided to tread the boards of the British stage and sailed for Liverpool in January of 1813.

America being then at war with England, Payne was, upon arrival, promptly imprisoned. He soon obtained release, however, thanks to family friends, and resumed his intended career as an actor. His English debut was again as Young Norval, at Drury Lane on June 4 of that year. He was an immediate success and played subsequently in other English cities and in Dublin.

Payne first traveled to Paris in 1815, where he was befriended by the great French actor Talma. He was received as a welcome visitor at the Comédie Française and became familiar with the contemporary French drama. Thus, he embarked upon a career as translator and adaptor of French melodramas for London's two principal theaters, Drury Lane and Covent Garden. It was in the years 1816 to 1832 that Payne wrote the bulk of his plays and established his international reputation as a dramatist. Most of his works premiered in London, with subsequent performances in various American cities.

Payne returned to his native America in July of 1832, after a career of playwriting abroad that had brought him much notoriety but little financial gain. His homecoming was observed with celebrations and testimonials, but America was not yet prepared to recognize its native dramatists with financial reward. Although his many plays were constantly performed throughout America (as many as twenty-five in a single season), he received virtually no remuneration for them aside from an occasional benefit performance.

After his return to America, Payne's career in the theater was virtually ended. He spent the remainder of his life working on behalf of the Cherokee Indians and serving in the capacity of Consul at Tunis under President Tyler. Payne died in Tunis on April 9, 1852.

Some sixty plays of varying importance have been attributed to Payne; only four of his major works can be mentioned here. *Brutus; or, The Fall of Tarquin* is a historical tragedy that was first acted at Drury Lane on December 3, 1818. It was to become one of Payne's more popular plays, receiving over fifty performances in its first season alone. Payne based the work upon five earlier plays by various dramatists on the subject of the ancient Roman patriot Brutus, creating a tragedy whose success was equalled by few plays in its time, English or American.

With *Brutus*, Payne contributed significantly to the advance of romanticism over classicism in European drama. It is interesting that the success of Payne's *Brutus* occurred twelve years before the appearance of Victor Hugo's much-noted *Hernani*, the play that is generally credited with toppling French neoclassicism. *Brutus* was played successfully in Paris and may well have influenced the young Hugo.

Brutus had its American premiere at the Park Theatre on March 15, 1819, and was popular on the American stage for seventy years, serving as a vehicle for such great tragedians as Edwin Forrest, John Mc-Cullough, and Edwin Booth. The original Brutus at Drury Lane had been Edmund Kean. Although Payne was accused of plagiarism in the composition of the play, he had freely acknowledged his debt to his sources, and the play testifies to his sense of the dramatic in his selecting, rearranging, and adapting from previous versions. The plain fact is that none of the five source plays had ever achieved even a modest success on its own.

Few people today have ever heard of Payne's *Clari; or, The Maid of Milan*, but virtually everyone knows "Home, Sweet Home," the song that Payne wrote for that drama. Indeed, the success of the song rivaled that of the play, which was one of Payne's great crowd-pleasers. *Clari* first appeared at Covent Garden on May 8, 1823, and was an instant success. It had its American premiere at the Park on November 12.

Clari is an operetta of the sentimental-melodrama variety, and its music was written by Henry Rowley Bishop, the distinguished British composer. Bishop and Payne wrote "Home, Sweet Home" as a song for Clari, the sweet young heroine of the piece; Bishop's melody then followed her throughout the work as a sort of leitmotif. Critical reactions to the operetta invariably focused upon this song, which was reviewed in such terms as "simple, sweet, touching, beyond any we almost ever heard." *Bell's Weekly Messenger* wrote of the song: "The ballad is entitled to every praise. It is simple and sweet and expressed the longing, lingering tenderness with which the heart reverts to its best affections."[3]

The success of *Clari* and of "Home, Sweet Home" vis-à-vis the financial gain they provided their creators makes a telling comment upon the status of the professional dramatist in the nineteenth century. The play was performed throughout England and America with enormous success for years, and the song was published separately in an edition of one hundred thousand copies the first year alone, yet neither Payne nor Bishop made a penny on the song. Payne's most recent biographer has determined that his total income from both the play and the song over the years was probably in the realm of $270. This deplorable situation was to plague American dramatists until roughly the end of the century, when international copyright laws would at last provide effective protection for the playwright.

Payne enjoyed a long and close friendship with Washington Irving; the two met probably in 1806. During their association, they collaborated on the writing of half a dozen plays, two of which were ultimately produced: *Charles the Second* and *Richelieu*. Irving's precise role in the composition of these plays is difficult to determine. His letters to Payne show that he modestly considered himself a minor collaborator, and he repeatedly expressed his reluctance to have his name connected with Payne's plays or to profit financially from them.

Charles the Second; or, The Merry Monarch was first acted at Covent Garden on May 27, 1824. Its American premiere was at the Park on October 25 that same year. It earned considerable success with its original audiences and is judged today the best of Payne's comedies, if not the best of all his plays. The comedy was adapted from a French play by Alexandre Duval (1760–1838), but Payne and Irving exercised considerable originality in the adaptation, including the addition of songs, set to music by H. R. Bishop, composer of "Home, Sweet Home."

Charles the Second is a three-act prose comedy of genuine fun and humor. The plot centers on the escapades of England's "merry monarch" in a single night's ramble. Charles is known throughout London and his court as a "wild devil." "He is a rover—rambles about at night—frolics in taverns" and is also a "desperate rogue among the petticoats." His cohort in his "rambling frolics" is the Earl of Rochester, who is in love with Lady Clara. At the entreaty of the Queen (who never appears in the play), Lady Clara promises Rochester that she will marry him, "if, by your ascendency over the king, you can disgust him with these nocturnal rambles, and bring him back to reason" (I, i).

Rochester agrees to the bargain and attempts to effect the King's reform by taking him to a tavern in Wapping, owned by Captain Copp, a salty rogue who has retired from the sea in order to adopt and rear his lovely niece, Mary. Mary is loved by Edward, the king's page, who courts her in the disguise of Georgini, a music master. When Rochester and the King arrive at the tavern, disguised as seamen, they encounter Edward, as well as Mary and Copp, and the disguises, misunderstandings, and cross-intrigues constitute the delightful situation that dominates the play's long second act.

Rochester encourages Charles to run up a large bill at the tavern, then absconds with the King's purse, leaving the not-so-merry monarch to answer the angry Copp. Charles daren't reveal his true identity and has no alternative but to offer to leave his diamond-studded watch with Copp as security against the debt. Copp realizes that the watch is too fine for a lowly sailor and believes Charles has stolen it. He locks the King in an upstairs room of the tavern and goes off for help. Rochester's ruse has had its effect. Charles, in a horrid predicament, soliloquizes: "Charles! Charles! Wilt thou never learn wisdom? Yes; let me but get out of *this* scrape, and I renounce these rambling humours forever" (II, ii).

Copp sends Mary and Edward, both armed, to

guard the "prisoner," but Charles is able, with the bribe of a ring, to convince them to allow his escape. At the climactic curtain of the act, Copp returns just in time to see Charles leap from the window to freedom, after stealing a kiss from Mary and shouting back to her to "tell uncle Copp to put it in the bill!" Copp fires his shotgun at the escaping monarch and the curtain falls.

In the brief third act, Copp and Mary come to the palace to return the King's watch and ring. It is here that a minor subplot is resolved; Rochester is revealed as the brother of Mary's mother and thus Mary's uncle. Mary and Copp recognize the King and Rochester, but are reluctant to expose their monarch— particularly so when he gives the watch to Copp and the ring to Mary and consents to her marriage with Edward. Thus all ends happily. Two marriages are in the offing, and the King, who has learned his lesson, asks them all to observe a "most profound secresy in regard to our whimsical adventures at Wapping" (III, i).

Charles the Second is delightful fare, a treat for the modern reader. Its emphasis is upon farcical fun, only occasionally dampened by touches of sentiment. It is carefully plotted to exact the maximum humor from its various mistaken identities. Its characters are clearly defined and sympathetically handled, and its dialogue is swift-moving and filled with good-natured jokes.

The character of Captain Copp offers much of the fun of the piece. He is reminiscent of an English "humours" character as he speaks of everything in terms of the sea. He explains to Mary his protective attitude: "Thou art all that's left to me out of the family fleet— a poor slight little pinnace. I've seen the rest, one after another, go down; it shall go hard but I'll convoy thee safe into port" (II, i). Copp also supplies a recurring gag that would appeal to any audience. He repeatedly attempts to sing a song that Mary refuses to allow him to complete, for obvious reasons. The song begins:

As old Admiral Trump,
In the time of the Rump,
With his broom swept the chops of the Channel:
And his crew of Tenbreeches,
Those Dutch sons of ——

—at which point Mary claps her hand over his mouth.

Payne and Irving's only other collaboration to be performed was *Richelieu, A Domestic Tragedy*, acted at Covent Garden on February 11, 1826, as *The French Libertine*. It too was adapted from a Duval play. *Richelieu* was not successful in its original production, chiefly for political reasons. The title character is the historical Duke of Richelieu, who is drawn in the play as a villainous libertine. Serving as the French ambassador to England at the time of the premiere was a descendant of the real Richelieu, who looked unkindly upon the denigration of his ancestor. He was able to mount a considerable cabal against the play, even though Charles Kemble, its producer, had changed the title and had altered the name of the central character to Rougemont.

The London press too was hostile to *Richelieu* and could not accept the style of exaggerated satire that Payne and Irving had concocted in delineating their libertine. The play was dubbed a "style of entertainment which we are not to see endured in this country" and the "kind of vulgar ribaldry which will not do for England."[4] *Richelieu* was given only six performances in London, although it was played with more success in America, being acted even as late as 1850. It is not so fine a play as *Charles the Second*, but it is worthy of note for Irving's collaborative influence.

In 1824 Irving wrote Payne that he would no longer be involved in the writing of plays and that their collaboration was, therefore, at an end. His reason must have struck Payne as all too just:

> I am sorry to say I cannot afford to write any more for the theatre. . . . The experiment has satisfied me that I should never at any time be compensated for my trouble. I speak not with reference to my talents, but to the market price my productions will command in other departments of literature.[5]

John Howard Payne, the most prolific American dramatist of his time, was, like his colleagues, in his words "never at any time . . . compensated" to the degree that his considerable talents warranted. He labored for nearly twenty years to enrich the coffers of British and American theatrical producers, but he lived his later years in virtual penury.

Anna Cora Mowatt Ritchie (1819–1870)

If Payne earns the credit for bringing international recognition to the American dramatist, he had a worthy successor in Anna Cora Mowatt Ritchie, an actress of immense popularity and author of the distinctive American comedy of manners, *Fashion* (1845). Her life story, recorded in detail in her *Autobiography of an Actress* (1854), is one of the more compelling accounts of theatrical life in mid-nineteenth-century America, and it reveals its author as a lady of intelligence, talent, and personal charm.

Anna Cora was born in Bordeaux, France, the daughter of Samuel Ogden, scion of an established New York family. As very young children, she and her siblings engaged in playacting. Her early fascination with the drama is evidenced by her own assertion that she had, by the age of ten, read all of Shakespeare's plays "many times over." She made her acting debut at the age of four, in a French-language version of *Othello*, staged in the family drawing room. Her autobiography preserves the account:

> My eldest sister enacted Desdemona; my eldest brother Othello; the second sister Emilia; the second brother Cassio, doubling the part with that of the uncle. . . . A difficulty occurred about the judges in the trial scene. Our dramatic corps proved insufficient to furnish judges. To supply this vacancy, the four younger children were summoned, dressed in red gowns and white wigs, made to sit on high benches, and instructed to pay great attention and not to laugh. Of these children I was the youngest; and at four years old in the sedate and solemn character of a judge, upon a mimic stage, I made my first appearance in that profession of which it was the permission of divine Providence that I should one day in reality become a member.[6]

When Anna Cora was six years old, her family returned to America, where the girl continued her dramatic activities by serving as impresario for frequent domestic theatricals, writing scripts and directing her brothers and sisters in a succession of drawing-room performances.

The young Miss Ogden's personal life was hardly less dramatic than her "theatrical" one. At the age of fifteen she brought off a romantic elopement with James Mowatt, a New York barrister, who remained her husband for seventeen years, until his death in 1851. Shortly after this marriage she fell victim to tuberculosis, an illness that was to plague her repeatedly for a number of years. At age eighteen she was sent to England for a cure. Her husband joined her there, her health improved, and the two returned to America in 1840.

It was at this time that Anna Cora Mowatt made her

first serious attempt at playwriting. The result was *Gulzara; or, The Persian Slave*, a drama that she wrote and produced as a family entertainment in celebration of her father's birthday in October, 1840. *Gulzara* was staged in the ballroom of the Ogdens' Flatbush home, and Anna Cora herself played the leading role. Since her brothers had declined to participate, she wrote the play for six female characters.

The authoress had spared no expense in obtaining elaborate scenes and costumes for the presentation, and the performance was attended by many representatives of New York society. *Gulzara*, of interest today chiefly as a curiosity, showed promise nonetheless. Epes Sargent, the author and journalist, wrote of it:

> There is a unity and simplicity in its design and execution which cannot fail to give sincere pleasure. It is pervaded by rare and delicate thought; many passages are strikingly beautiful, and the impartial critic will think, with us, that the drama would do credit to a much more experienced writer.[7]

For the next few years, Anna Cora enjoyed a successful career as a platform reader and a magazinist. She contributed articles to such periodicals as *Godey's Lady's Book* and *Graham's Magazine* under the nom de plume of Helen Berkley. She wrote a prizewinning novel, *The Fortune Hunter*, in 1842, and in 1845 her dramatic masterpiece, *Fashion*, was acted in New York.

Mrs. Mowatt wrote *Fashion* at the urging of Epes Sargent, a longtime friend of the Ogden family. Sargent was acquainted with the management of the Park Theatre and was instrumental in getting the play produced there. *Fashion* was, therefore, accorded a first-rate cast and an elaborate physical production.

The author was well known among the New York

elite, and the premiere of her first comedy on March 24, 1845, attracted considerable attention. In fact, the opening-night audience was composed of a class of spectators seldom seen at the Park. The cream of New York society, headed by the John Jacob Astors, turned out to appraise Mrs. Mowatt's efforts. Even the third tier, usually the province of prostitutes, was populated instead by more respectable auditors— students and stockbrokers.

The play was a smashing success. It ran for twenty nights in succession, and the press accorded it an unprecedented volume of attention, almost uniformly favorable. According to Mrs. Mowatt's most recent biographer: "No play ever written by an American is comparable to *Fashion* in the immediate sensation which it created or its long-range effects on the course of American drama. . . . With *Fashion* the drama as an *art* had its birth in America."[8]

It was shortly after the success of *Fashion* that Anna Cora Mowatt made the decision to become an actress. She took to the boards more out of financial necessity than artistic design; her husband's business ventures had failed and she hoped to secure a living from acting. Her career, although brief, was brilliant.

She made her debut as Pauline in Bulwer-Lytton's *The Lady of Lyons* at the Park Theatre on June 13, 1845. With the help of the actor W. H. Crisp, Mrs. Mowatt, who knew little or nothing about acting, had undertaken a program of self-training and had learned in a few short weeks what other actors had devoted lifetimes to mastering. Her work paid off; she was a dazzling success. The Park was filled once again with one of the most distinguished audiences it had ever accommodated and all agreed that her Pauline was a triumph.

During the first year alone of her acting career, Anna Cora Mowatt gave some two hundred performances, repeating her successful *Lady of Lyons* role and introducing new ones into her repertoire. Her reputation spread quickly throughout America, and in 1846 she took the popular actor E. L. Davenport as her leading man. He remained in this capacity until her retirement in 1854.

It was for herself and Davenport that Anna Cora Mowatt wrote her only other major play, *Armand, the Child of the People*. It opened at the Park Theatre on September 27, 1847, to considerable acclaim, and was played subsequently also in Boston. *Armand* is a romantic drama, partly in blank verse, set in the period of Louis XV of France. It seems today quite conventional and melodramatic, but it serves to place Anna Cora Mowatt the dramatist squarely in the midst of the romantic tradition of Payne, Bird, Boker, and the other leading playwrights of her time.

In 1847 Mrs. Mowatt and Davenport made their English debut in Manchester, and in the following year they appeared in London. London playgoers were customarily cool to American actors. Edwin Forrest had offended British sensibilities with his flamboyant, muscular style of playing during his London appearances in 1836. Thus, Mrs. Mowatt met with considerable hostility from her fellow players while rehearsing for her London debut as Julia in Sheridan Knowles's *The Hunchback*. The actors at the Princess's Theatre lost no opportunity to tell Mrs. Mowatt how the leading London actresses had performed the role of Julia. At one point, Anna Cora lost her composure and told one of the actors: "Sir, when I have made up my mind to become the mere imitator of Mrs. Butler, or of Miss Faucit, or of Mrs. Kean, I shall come to *you* for instruction. At present it is for the public to decide upon the faultiness of my conception."[9] And decide they did. Anna Cora Mowatt was warmly received by the London audiences and critics

Fashion. Produced by the Yale School of Drama in 1963. Directed by Curtis Canfield; settings by Robert E. Darling; costumes by Richard Anderson.

YALE SCHOOL OF DRAMA LIBRARY, PHOTO: A. BURTON STREET

alike, who found her acting refined and charming. *The Theatrical Times* wrote that she was a "decided acquisition to the theatre, being free from coarseness and Americanisms."[10]

Mrs. Mowatt and Davenport remained in the British Isles until 1851, playing Ireland and Scotland as well as the English cities. It was while she was in Scotland, in 1851, that the actress received word of the death of her husband, James. She returned to America at once.

After her return, Anna Cora Mowatt achieved a series of successes on the stages of America's major cities: New York, St. Louis, Boston, Buffalo, New Orleans, and so on. Then in 1854, after only nine years as an actress, Anna Cora Mowatt retired from the stage and married William F. Ritchie, a Richmond gentleman. She continued to publish fiction in her later years and lived chiefly abroad after 1861. She died in London on July 28, 1870.

Mrs. Mowatt's *Fashion; or, Life in New York* is the definitive American comedy of manners of the nineteenth century, just as Tyler's *The Contrast* had been that of the preceding century. There are similarities, in fact, between the two plays, although *Fashion* is the more complex and more incisive of the two. It is significant that Mrs. Mowatt's comedy is even today played in college and university theaters and was successfully revived in New York in 1924, in 1959, and, most recently, in a musical adaptation in 1974.

The play is set in the New York of Mrs. Mowatt's own time. The central figure is Mrs. Tiffany, a pretentious, social-climbing matron who affects all that is foreign and fashionable and deplores the gaucheries of native American manners. Mrs. Tiffany, a former milliner who married into wealth, has procured the services of a French maid, Millinette, to coach her in French manners and fashions. She has also decked out her colored servant, Zeke, in elegant livery in an attempt to pass him off as a French footman. Regular visitors to the Tiffany home include T. Tennyson Twinkle, an affected poet of no talent; Augustus Fogg, a "drawing room appendage" who affects indifference toward everyone and everything (except food); and Count Jolimaitre, a bogus French nobleman whom Mrs. Tiffany virtually worships and whose sole aim is to marry into the Tiffany money.

Mrs. Tiffany, thinking Jolimaitre wealthy and titled, wants to marry her daughter, Seraphina, to him, but her design is foiled by her husband, Mr. Tiffany, a merchant who has committed embezzlement and is being blackmailed by his clerk, Snobson. Snobson too wants to marry into the Tiffany money by wedding Seraphina, and to this end he threatens to expose Tiffany's crime unless he promotes the match. Also resident in the Tiffany household are Prudence, Mrs. Tiffany's sensible sister, and Gertrude, Seraphina's shy and mysterious governess.

The Tiffanys are visited by Adam Trueman, a plain-spoken, rustic septuagenarian and longtime friend of Mr. Tiffany. Trueman constantly points out the hypocrisy of the Tiffany household and denounces the affectation of foreign manners. He favors honest, native American ways. He seems particularly interested in Gertrude the governess, the only seemingly sincere member of the household, even though Gertrude has a partiality for the manly Colonel Howard, an officer in the United States Army.

Mrs. Tiffany throws a gala ball, during which event all of the intrigues of the plot come to a crisis. Jolimaitre is exposed by Millinette as a fraud—a fortune-hunting con artist rather than a count. Jolimaitre thus loses Seraphina and is claimed by Millinette. Snobson's blackmail of Mr. Tiffany backfires when Trueman points out that the clerk is an accessory after the fact and, therefore, is as guilty as his employer. Snobson backs down and decides to move to California(!). The crowning discovery, however, is that Gertrude is the long-lost granddaughter of Adam Trueman and therefore an heiress. Trueman bestows his granddaughter's hand upon Colonel Howard and dictates to Mr. Tiffany the necessary expiation for his crime and for his wife's foolishness:

> You must sell your house and all these gew gaws, and bundle your wife and daughter off to the country. There let them learn economy, true independence, and home virtues, instead of foreign follies. As for yourself, continue your business— but let moderation, in future, be your counsellor, and let *honesty* be your confidential clerk.
>
> (V, i)

The story line of *Fashion* is trivial, artificial, and conventional; its plot is dependent upon concealed identities, deception, and coincidence. The comedy's strength lies in its delightful characterizations and its incisive commentary upon pretension and affectation.

Like *The Contrast*, *Fashion* pits native American worth against foreign influence, arriving at the sound conclusion that America has no need to emulate her European cousins.

Mrs. Tiffany is the pivotal character, and she is hilariously absurd in her passion for fashion. Her speech is peppered with fractured French; she claims that "there is something about our American words decidedly vulgar" (I, i). Her insistence upon calling her armchair a "fow-tool" *(fauteuil)* becomes a recurring joke throughout the comedy. When her sister reminds Mrs. Tiffany of her past as a milliner, she responds: "Forget what we *have* been, it is enough to remember that we *are* of the *upper ten thousand*" (I, i). On the subject of her age, she claims: "A woman of fashion *never* grows old! Age is always out of fashion" (I, i). It is Mrs. Tiffany's expensive indulgence in fashion that has forced her husband to commit embezzlement.

Count Jolimaitre too is a skillfully drawn comic character. Mrs. Tiffany describes him as "decidedly the most fashionable foreigner in town," but we know from the first that he is a fraud. When Millinette first sees him she screams in recognition; he is her old pal Gustave Treadmill. Although Jolimaitre affects a disdain for all that is American, he admits to "one redeeming charm in America—the superlative loveliness of the feminine portion of creation,—(*Aside*.) and the wealth of their obliging papas" (I, i). Trueman and Colonel Howard are the only two who see through Jolimaitre's pretensions; the latter describes him as a "puppy of a Count—that paste jewel thrust upon the little finger of society" (IV, i).

Although Mrs. Tiffany dominates the comic world of *Fashion*, the "hero" of the piece is clearly Adam Trueman. In him, Mrs. Mowatt personified the ideal of American manhood. His role, like that of Colonel Manly in *The Contrast*, is to reflect upon the hypocrisy and artificiality of the play's fashionable figures. Trueman does not mince words. At his first entrance he deplores the sight of Zeke in his servant's livery and protests to Mrs. Tiffany: "To make men wear the *badge of servitude* in a free land,—that's the fashion, is it? Hurrah, for republican simplicity!" (I, i) He later admonishes Mr. Tiffany: "This *fashion*-worship has made heathens and hypocrites of you all! *Deception* is your household God!" (II, i) His definitive pronouncement on fashion is made to Mrs. Tiffany at the height of her gala ball:

> Fashion! And pray what is *fashion*, madam? An agreement between certain persons to live without using their souls! to substitute etiquette for virtue —decorum for purity—manners for morals! to affect a shame for the works of their Creator! and expend all their rapture upon the works of their tailors and dressmakers!
>
> (IV, i)

It is undoubtedly in the voice of Adam Trueman that Mrs. Mowatt expressed her faith in the efficacy of a truly American society—a society in which she herself functioned with admirable grace and considerable success.

Anna Cora Mowatt Ritchie's fame as a dramatist rests today upon a single play. Her brilliant career as an actress lasted a mere nine years, and few today who have heard of *Fashion* are even aware that its author was one of the brightest stars on the American stage. Nevertheless, her contributions to the theater were considerable. She wrote what remains today the definitive American comedy of manners before 1900. She proved that a gentlewoman of taste and breeding could function in the world of the theater without demeaning herself, thus adding respectability to the profession. And she served notice to the world that America was capable of producing dramatists and actors of consummate skill.

6. THE ROMANTIC MOVEMENT

If American plays from the first third of the nine-teenth century were notable for their melodramatic plots and patriotic sentiments, those of the following three decades continued the highly romantic mode that John Howard Payne had introduced in his dramas of *Brutus* and *Richelieu*. American drama of the 1830s, 1840s, and 1850s generally reflects the romantic move-ment in literature that dominated both European and American letters at that time.

The period was also one in which the theatergoer's attention was diverted somewhat from the drama as literature, to be focused instead on the art of the actor. American acting came into its own in the middle of the nineteenth century, and a play's success was mea-sured not so much by the excellence of the script as it was by the charismatic performance of the actor who projected it across the footlights. This was the period of popular actors like Junius Brutus Booth (1796–1852) and the great Edwin Forrest (1806–1872), and of actresses of great charm and appeal, such as Mary Ann Duff (1794–1857) and Charlotte Cushman (1816–1876). These American actors and their col-leagues developed great skill in the declamatory and flamboyant performance style so well suited to works from the classical repertoire as well as to the new plays written for their special talents.

In general, the American plays written at this time appear to us as poor imitations of Shakespeare, but there were a few dramas of genuine merit that deserve the attention of the modern reader. Among the playwrights who produced them, at least two may be considered major dramatists of their time: Robert Montgomery Bird and George Henry Boker.

Robert Montgomery Bird (1806–1854)

The name of Robert Montgomery Bird is traditionally linked with that of Edwin Forrest, the first great American actor. Bird's career as a dramatist was initiated and sustained by Forrest, who found in the writer a source of dramatic material that would display his histrionic abilities to the full. Their association, at first mutually productive and congenial, lasted a mere six years, however, and their parting was marked by bitterness and rancor. Despite the encouragement that Forrest gave him, Bird was clearly the victim of the great tragedian's unscrupulous business dealings.

Bird was born on February 5, 1806, in New Castle, Delaware. His father died when he was four, and the boy was brought up in the household of his uncle, in an atmosphere of refinement and cultural awareness. The young Bird attended the New Castle Academy and, later, the Germantown Academy in Philadelphia. In 1824 he entered the School of Medicine at the University of Pennsylvania, receiving his M.D. degree in 1827. It is for this reason that history frequently refers to him as "Dr. Bird."

His medical degree notwithstanding, Bird abandoned the practice of medicine after only a year and turned to literary pursuits. In the years 1827 and 1828 he contributed verse and stories to the *Philadelphia Monthly Magazine* and wrote five plays (none of which was produced), as well as a considerable body of dramatic fragments. Since he kept fairly complete notebooks of his literary activities from 1826 on, we know that he read voraciously and was familiar with the Elizabethan and Restoration dramatists, to whose works his own plays bear some resemblance.

Bird's association with Forrest began in 1830, when the actor offered a cash prize for an American play that he could add to his repertoire. Bird won the prize with his *Pelopidas*, which Forrest accepted but never acted. Instead, Forrest encouraged Bird to write a second play for him. The result was *The Gladiator* (1831), a play that was, according to Arthur Hobson Quinn, the "most successful so far performed in America."[1]

Subsequently, Bird also provided for Forrest the plays *Oralloossa* (1832), *The Broker of Bogota* (1834), and a rewrite of John Augustus Stone's 1829 drama *Metamora* (1836). *The Gladiator*, *Oralloossa*, and *The Broker of Bogota* remained in Forrest's repertoire throughout his career and brought him considerable wealth. Bird's total return from these three plays was $3,000, for which paltry sum he surrendered his rights to the manuscripts. Forrest not only refused to further remunerate Bird for the works but also prohibited him from publishing the plays. This unhappy state of affairs came to a head in 1837, when Forrest had the temerity to accuse Bird of defaulting on a personal loan. The misunderstanding led Bird to end his association with Forrest and abandon writing for the theater.

In the years 1834 through 1839, Bird wrote five novels, the best known of which is *Nick of the Woods*

(1837). In his later years he edited the Philadelphia *North American* magazine, tended his farm in Delaware, and served in political offices for the Whig party. Throughout his life, Robert Montgomery Bird was respected by all who knew him as an extraordinarily versatile and scholarly gentleman. He exemplified the "Renaissance man" of the new American society and he did much to lend respectability to American letters. He died in Philadelphia on January 23, 1854.

Bird's first five plays are clearly apprentice work and offer little for the modern reader.[2] They are interesting chiefly as proof that their author was familiar with the classic English plays and could extract from them the essential principles of dramatic composition. Although none of the five was acted, all evidence a remarkable sense of theatricality for an author who was just over twenty years of age at the time of their composition.

Bird did not write *Pelopidas; or, The Fall of the Polemarchs* expressly for Forrest, but the actor chose it nevertheless as the recipient of his cash prize for a new American play in 1830. It is a romantic verse tragedy based upon Plutarch's account of the revolt of the Theban city against the tyrants of Sparta. Although Forrest awarded his prize to *Pelopidas*, he never produced it, probably because the roles of Philadas the Theban patriot and Sibylla, Pelopidas' wife, are more interesting than that of Pelopidas. Forrest may have feared that he would not shine sufficiently as the hero.

As a substitute for *Pelopidas*, therefore, Bird wrote for Forrest the play that was to become one of the most successful tragedies in the history of American drama, *The Gladiator* (Park Theatre, September 26, 1831). This romantic verse tragedy depicts the uprising of the Roman slaves under the leadership of Spartacus, a Thracian gladiator. The role of Spartacus was perfect both for Forrest's flamboyant, declamatory style and for his muscular physique; it became the greatest role of his career. By 1853 he had acted Spartacus a thousand times, and he continued to play it until his retirement in 1872, after which various other tragedians adopted it, keeping Bird's play on the boards until the turn of the century.

A month after the original New York performance, Forrest took *The Gladiator* to Philadelphia's Arch Street Theatre, where it drew the largest audience ever assembled there and received the tribute of a standing ovation. The Philadelphia actor F. C. Wemyss wrote of this performance:

> I was taken by surprise at the effect produced at the closing of the second Act. The rising of the Gladiators in the arena, and the disposition of the characters as the Act drop fell, I do not believe was ever surpassed in any theatre in the world.[3]

Forrest acted *The Gladiator* for his London debut at Drury Lane, October 17, 1836, with great success. The London *Courier* wrote of Bird's play: "America has at length vindicated her capability of producing a dramatist of the highest order, whose claims should be unequivocally acknowledged by the Mother Country."[4] As a result of the London success of *The Gladiator*, Bird was elected an honorary member of London's Dramatic Authors' Society in 1836.

For American audiences, the appeal of *The Gladiator* undoubtedly lay in its themes of freedom from oppression and the dignity of the common man. Spartacus is a Thracian slave of simple nobility and strength, who battles oppression and subjugation by the ruling aristocracy. Slavery was a subject of immediate concern to Americans in the 1830s, and Bird himself acknowledged: "If *The Gladiator* were produced in a slave state, the managers, players, and perhaps myself in the bargain, would be rewarded with the Penitentiary!"[5]

Bird's next play for Forrest was not nearly so successful, nor is it so effective a drama as *The Gladiator*. *Oralloossa, Son of the Incas* premiered at Philadelphia's Arch Street Theatre on October 10, 1832, and was subsequently played by Forrest only intermittently for the next fifteen years. It is a romantic tragedy of Peruvian history, recounting the assassination of Pizarro. Bird combined historical fact with imaginative fiction in fashioning his plot, and the principal appeal of the play lay in its capitalizing on the Indian-play tradition, which was so popular at the time.

Oralloossa was followed by *The Broker of Bogota*, generally considered to be Bird's masterpiece. It opened at New York's Bowery Theatre on February 12, 1834, and remained in Forrest's repertoire throughout his career. On the night of its premiere, Forrest sent Bird a letter that read in part: "I have just left the theatre—your tragedy was performed and crowned with entire success. 'The Broker of Bogota' will live when our vile trunks are rotten. You have every reason to congratulate yourself."[6]

Unlike Bird's other serious plays, *The Broker of Bogota* is a domestic drama; for once, the dramatist turned from the exoticism of ancient Thebes, Rome, and Peru. The setting is Santa Fe de Bogotá in New Granada, presumably in the eighteenth century. The broker of the title is Baptista Febro, a middle-class moneylender who is the "richest man in Bogota."

At the play's opening, Febro has disowned his eldest son, Ramon, a profligate youth who has been led astray by his companion, Antonio de Cabarero, the "villain that seduced him into folly." Ramon loves Juana, daughter of a neighboring merchant, Mendoza, but his hopes of winning her hand are dashed by his disinheritance. Mendoza will not permit his daughter to marry Ramon. Febro's daughter, Leonor, meanwhile, is courted by Fernando, the son of Granada's Viceroy, who woos her in disguise as one Rolando (for reasons never entirely made clear).

Ramon, in his dissipation, has become deeply indebted to Pablo, a ne'er-do-well innkeeper and accomplice of Cabarero. Thus, his hopes, both romantic and social, depend upon his acquiring some money. Cabarero urges the youth to rob his own father. Ramon is, throughout the action, torn between his love for his father and his involvement with Cabarero. Old Febro too is torn between rejecting his son and providing the money that will free the boy from Cabarero's clutches.

Cabarero visits Febro to try to extort money from him, but the broker becomes enraged and, with bitter irony, invites the villain to rob him, crying: "If thou wilt more, there's money in my vaults;/Break them, and rob me! . . ./Rob me, thou knave, that I may have thy life!" (I, iii). This confrontation is overheard by the servant, Silvano, who is not too bright and takes his master's words at face value.

Cabarero too takes the invitation literally and, upon conveniently finding a lost key to Febro's vaults, robs the broker, with the assistance of Pablo and Ramon. Meanwhile, Febro, unaware of the robbery, has a change of heart and decides to take a bag of gold to his son at Pablo's inn. He arrives just as the thieving triumvirate are attempting to hide their booty. When pursuing officers arrive on the scene and see both the stolen loot and Febro with the bag of gold in his hands, Cabarero cleverly accuses Febro of "self-robbery." His accusation is backed by Pablo, and Ramon remains silent, refusing to establish his father's innocence.

The Broker of Bogota. The great Edwin Forrest as Febro, with Miss Lilli as Leonor.

Febro is tried by the Viceroy for robbing his own vaults, and found guilty. Disgraced and desolate, he returns home only to discover that his daughter, Leonor, has run off with her "Rolando." Juana meanwhile forces from Ramon the truth about the robbery, renounces him, and runs to inform the Viceroy of Febro's innocence and of the villainy of the nefarious trio: Cabarero, Pablo, and Ramon.

In the final scene, Febro comes to the Viceroy's

palace in search of his daughter and her paramour. Juana arrives and exposes the villainous robbery plot. Leonor and "Rolando" arrive and the latter is revealed to be the Viceroy's son. Pablo, threatened with torture, confesses all, confirming Cabarero's and Ramon's villainy. Ramon, disgraced and rejected by all, rushes from the room. A single ray of happiness, the union of Leonor and Fernando, is snuffed out by the news that Ramon has thrown himself from the balcony. Old Febro falls to the floor, his heart broken.

Like most of the serious American plays of its time, *The Broker of Bogota* imitates the language and tone of Elizabethan tragedy. It is written in an alternation of prose and blank verse (with no apparent system to the shifts) and its dialogue, frequently bombastic, is filled with "thee," "thy," "thou hadst," " 'slife," "sirrah," "methinks," and other terms utterly foreign to nineteenth-century American speech.

Bird's familiarity with Shakespeare is evident throughout the play. The relationship between Ramon and Cabarero recalls the Bertram–Parolles situation of *All's Well That Ends Well.* Cabarero is a thoroughgoing Machiavel, in the tradition of *Othello*'s Iago, although his humorous comments and swaggering insouciance make him a most appealing character. There are echoes, too, of Shylock in old Febro, although Bird's moneylender is from the first a respected member of the community. It is clear that his love for his children outweighs his concern for wealth.

The Broker of Bogota exhibits the usual structural flaws of the romantic melodrama of its time. Fernando's disguise as Rolando is but weakly motivated, appearing as disguise merely for the sake of convention, and the discovery of his true identity comes so late as to render the whole intrigue somewhat confusing to a theater audience. Eavesdropping and misunderstanding make their wonted contribution to the action. Accidents and coincidence abound: the lost key to Febro's vault, an incriminating rosary dropped by Ramon at the scene of the robbery, and so on.

Nevertheless, *The Broker of Bogota* is unquestionably one of the outstanding American plays of its time. Its central characters are skillfully delineated, and their involvements are compelling and convincing. Bird's management of blank verse is excellent and his imagery frequently stunning, as in the Viceroy's warning to the accused Febro:

> Febro, attend: thy star is darkening fast;
> And the old trunk, whose wealthy branches hid
> The secret rot that hollowed at its heart,
> Is trembling in the tempest. Lo, the bolt
> Comes to the earth, and hisses at thy front
> A moment, ere it fells thee.
>
> (IV, i)

Finally, the drama contains some acting scenes of real substance—scenes rarely matched in the drama of the time, either American or English. It is easy to imagine the impact that Forrest must have had as Febro in this finest of Bird's dramas.

Bird's final play for Forrest was *Metamora*, the full text of which has not survived. Forrest had appeared with great success in a play of the same title by John Augustus Stone in 1829, and the actor commissioned Bird to revise the play in 1836. From the fragments that survive, it is evident that Bird's work was more a new treatment of the Indian theme than a simple rewrite of Stone's play. Nevertheless, Forrest never acted Bird's *Metamora*, nor did he compensate the dramatist for the work. When Bird asked Forrest to return the single existing copy of *Metamora* to him, the actor claimed to have misplaced it. It was shortly after this that the professional relationship, and the personal friendship, between Edwin Forrest and Robert Montgomery Bird came to its unpleasant end.

Bird did much to advance the vogue for romantic drama in America, and he endowed the genre with a high degree of artistry. Although he used exotic settings and historical events in the composition of a neo-Elizabethan style of tragedy, he dramatized themes that touched the American heart and mind: rebellion against oppressive tyranny, the pursuit of liberty, and the right of the individual to determine his own fate in a free society. "His plays," wrote Quinn, "mark a decided advance in the progress of our drama."[7]

George Henry Boker (1823–1890)

The romantic tradition in American drama reached its culmination in the works of George Henry Boker, author of the finest American tragedy before 1900, *Francesca da Rimini* (1855). Boker was among the few American dramatists who devoted their careers almost exclusively to literary production, and he followed the lead of writers like Bird and Payne in essaying the style of romantic period drama that appealed to the audiences of the mid-nineteenth century. Quinn called him "one of the greatest of our dramatists."[8]

Boker was born into a wealthy and cultivated Philadelphia family on October 6, 1823. His father, English by birth, was a successful Philadelphia banker, and young Boker never wanted for material comfort. It was this financial independence that allowed him eventually to pursue a literary career.

At the age of fifteen, Boker entered the College of New Jersey (now Princeton), graduating in 1842. Two years later he married and thereafter embarked upon a year-long European tour. Although he had studied law, he found it of little interest, and upon his return from Europe he made the decision to become a writer. In 1848 he published his first volume of verses and wrote his first play, *Calaynos*.

It was in the years 1849 to roughly 1855 that Boker dedicated himself primarily to the drama. He wrote eleven full-length plays, six of which were professionally produced. Almost every one was written in verse and set in some remote historical period and some foreign land. Boker's plays are, in fact, almost totally free from American themes and concerns. His tastes were decidedly classic, as his advice to a fellow writer, Richard Henry Stoddard, attests: "Read Chaucer for strength, read Spenser for ease and sweetness, read Milton for sublimity, read Shakespeare for all these things and for something else which is his alone. Get out of your age as far as you can."[9] Nevertheless, the universality of his themes, his skillful character drawing, and his facility with dramatic verse appealed greatly to American audiences.

After 1855, Boker turned to lyric poetry, producing a body of American verse that is among the best of the period. Even during his playwriting years, Boker considered himself primarily a poet, and accepted the theatrical aspect of his efforts as a mere by-product of his art. He wrote in a letter to Bayard Taylor in 1854: "My theatrical success I never valued. I had not, nor have I, any ambition to become a mere playwright. . . . If I could not be acknowledged as a poet, I had no further desire, and no further active concern in literature."[10]

During the Civil War years Boker devoted his efforts, as a civilian, to the cause of preserving the Union, writing patriotic verses and heading the influential Union League. He also gave public readings of his verses; he was once called by the actor Edwin Forrest the best reader in America.

The decade of the 1870s saw Boker in a diplomatic role. In 1871 he was appointed Minister to Turkey, and in 1875 he was promoted to Envoy to Russia. In the latter capacity he was well received by Emperor

Alexander II of Russia and did much to improve Russo-American relations. He returned to America in 1878.

The final ten years of Boker's life were characterized by a rekindling of his interest in the drama, sparked no doubt by the enormously successful revival of his *Francesca da Rimini* in 1882. His last two plays were written in this period, although neither was acted. His final years were clouded by recurring illness, and he died of a heart attack in Philadelphia, January 2, 1890.

Boker's eleven plays exhibit considerable variety of approach to playwriting: comedy and tragedy, blank verse and prose, historical and contemporary. It is obvious, however, that the dramatist's forte was historical verse tragedy; when he departed from that genre, the results were less successful.

The five unacted plays are generally inferior to the six that were produced. It is only the final two of these five, *Nydia* (1885) and *Glaucus* (1886), that might interest a modern reader. Both plays, which depict the destruction of Pompeii, are based upon Bulwer-Lytton's *The Last Days of Pompeii* (1834). The plays are quite similar and the relationship between the two is not clear.

Boker wrote *Nydia* at the urging of the actor Lawrence Barrett, who had achieved much success in the 1882 revival of *Francesca da Rimini*. It is probable that Barrett, unhappy with *Nydia*, asked Boker to rewrite the play and give added emphasis to the leading male role, that of Glaucus. The change of title, as well as the texts, support this assumption. In any case, Barrett had asked Boker to write for him a play that would provide a number of "gorgeous spectacular effects . . . something that would give the ingenuity of the stage carpenter, the scene painter and the costumer a chance."[11] The result was *Glaucus*.

Barrett never produced the play, although it is one

of Boker's better efforts. It provides, too, the opportunity for spectacle that the actor had requested. The
final stage direction, for example, reads in part:

> Flames and dense smoke bursts from Vesuvius.
> Loud rumbling sounds are heard. The columns
> of the temples reel and fall. The arch and cornice
> of the Basilica fall upon Arbaces and the Praetor.
> The people flee in every direction. A tremendous
> din, and crash of falling buildings goes on.

The first play by George Henry Boker to be acted
was *Calaynos*, a tragedy in blank verse that gives a
clear indication of its author's feeling for dramatic
poetry. It was first produced at London's Sadler's
Wells Theatre in an unauthorized, pirated version in
1849. (Prior to the establishment of international
copyright laws, a dramatist had no protection against
such piracy.) Its first American performance was at
the Walnut Street Theatre in Philadelphia, January 20,
1851, where it ran for eleven nights, a respectable
record for a native tragedy. *Calaynos* was sufficiently
popular that the actor James E. Murdoch was able to
claim, in 1864, that he had acted it at least fifty times
in Philadelphia, Baltimore, Albany, and Chicago.

Boker's next effort was not so successful. *The Be-
trothal*, a romantic comedy set in Renaissance Italy,
premiered at the Walnut Street on September 25,
1850, and was revived at New York's Broadway Theatre two months later. When it was played in England
in 1853, it met with considerable hostility from the
British press. Boker claimed, however, that the English
audiences had responded warmly and that the un-
favorable notices only confirmed the prejudice with
which the British press customarily greeted American
plays.

The third Boker play to reach the stage was *The
World a Mask* (Walnut Street Theatre, April 21,
1851), in which the playwright turned from historical

settings to contemporary social satire. The play is set in the London of Boker's time and is written mostly in prose. It serves to confirm Boker's weakness in comic writing. He himself evidently thought little of it, for he omitted it from the 1856 edition of his plays.

In his next produced play, Boker returned to historical tragedy—with happy results. *Leonor de Guzman*, among the best of Boker's plays, was quite well received. Its initial production was at the Walnut Street on October 3, 1853, where its run was limited to six nights, but only because of prior commitments of the theater. Of this production Boker wrote: "The tragedy was triumphant—well noticed by the press and increasing in public favor up to its last night."[12] It was even more successful in its New York performances six months later. *Leonor de Guzman*, set in Castile in 1350, is based upon actual personages and historical events. In it, Boker achieved his highest level of character drawing to date.

The merits of *Leonor de Guzman* were exceeded two years later by *Francesca da Rimini*, Boker's masterpiece and the finest American drama to that time. It opened at New York's Broadway Theatre on September 26, 1855. According to his own account, Boker wrote the play in a frenzy of inspiration, working night and day and completing the work in a mere three weeks.

Francesca da Rimini is a verse tragedy set in the neighboring cities of Ravenna and Rimini around 1300. Boker's inspiration was the account of the Paolo–Francesca love affair from the fifth canto of Dante's *Inferno*. (Dante himself is referred to in the play, somewhat mockingly, as the resident poet of Ravenna.) The story was well known and Boker's play was not the first to treat the subject in dramatic form. It was, however, the first in English and remains even today the best of all dramatic versions.

The plot of the tragedy is simple in its outline;

Boker avoided complicated storytelling in favor of extensive development of his characters' motivations and interactions. The background of the tragedy is the longtime feud between Lord Malatesta of Rimini and Guido da Polenta, Lord of Ravenna. In an attempt to lay to rest the animosity between the two cities, these princes agree to a marriage between Lanciotto, Malatesta's older son, and Francesca, the beautiful daughter of Guido. It is strictly a political marriage; the young couple have never seen each other.

Lanciotto, whom Boker makes the central figure of his tragedy, is a brave and renowned warrior but is also, unfortunately, a hunchback. He is painfully conscious of his deformity, describing himself as:

> The great twisted monster of the wars,
> The brawny cripple, the herculean dwarf,
> The spur of panic, and the butt of scorn.
>
> (I, ii)

Although he desperately craves love, Lanciotto fears even to meet, much less to wed, the beautiful Francesca, "whom the minstrels sing about," feeling certain that she will find him repulsive. Lanciotto's anxiety is heightened by the continual taunting of Pepe, Malatesta's jester. Pepe serves as a comic but sinister reminder to Lanciotto of his pathetic deformity. Lanciotto firmly believes himself to be a "most conspicuous monster" (I, iii).

Thus, Lanciotto arranges to send his younger brother, Paolo, as his envoy to claim the intended bride from Ravenna and bring her back to Rimini. Paolo and Lanciotto are very close, even though Lanciotto envies his brother's handsome physique. Paolo is, to his brother:

> the delight of Rimini,
> The pride and conscious centre of all eyes,

The theme of poets, the ideal of art,
The earthly treasury of Heaven's best gifts!
                                    (I, ii)

In Ravenna, meanwhile, everyone but Francesca, it
seems, is aware of Lanciotto's disfigurement, and they
all express pity for the unfortunate girl, who is, by her
own father's admission, "a sacrifice, I know,—/A limb
delivered to the surgeon's knife,/To save our general
health" (II, i). Afraid to inform his daughter of her
intended groom's deformity, the devious Guido allows
her to believe that the envoy from Rimini is Lanciotto
himself. When Paolo arrives, attended with great pomp
and ceremony, Francesca falls in love with him at first
sight, and he in turn is struck by her beauty.

Francesca soon learns, however, of her father's deception; the handsome youth she nearly gave her heart
to is not her intended husband. She bravely vows to
conceal her true feelings and return with Paolo to
Rimini to wed his brother, the hunchback Lanciotto.
Francesca puts her duty to family and city above the
dictates of her heart.

Upon meeting Lanciotto, she makes a noble effort
to love the misshapen warrior, but her passion for
Paolo will not subside. The sensitive Lanciotto, painfully aware that in spite of her willingness to wed him
she does not love him, is tortured by feelings of inade-
quacy. Nevertheless, politics prevail and the wedding
takes place.

Before the marriage can be consummated, however,
Lanciotto is suddenly called to the battlefield to re-
pulse the invading Ghibellines, and Francesca is left in
the care of Paolo. The outcome is predictable; Francesca and Paolo succumb to their mutual passion and
engage in an adulterous union. Their affair is overheard
by Pepe, who rushes to the battlefield to inform
Lanciotto of his new role as cuckold and to taunt him

Lawrence Barrett as Count Lanciotto in the 1882 revival of
Francesca da Rimini.

mercilessly. Lanciotto, infuriated with Pepe's tale of
his wife's infidelity, stabs the jester. As he is dying,
Pepe shows him a dagger belonging to Paolo (which he
had earlier stolen) and swears that Paolo had sent him
to murder Lanciotto. Pepe dies before Lanciotto can
get the truth from him, and the soldier rushes back
to the palace at Rimini to confront the adulterous pair.

Francesca da Rimini. Photograph of the 1901 Otis Skinner revival, with Skinner (*kneeling*) as Lanciotto, Aubrey Boucicault (*left of Skinner*) as Paolo, and Marcia Van Dresser (*right*) as Francesca.

In a deeply moving final scene, Lanciotto begs Paolo and Francesca to deny their guilt, but the couple prefer death to a renunciation of their love. Lanciotto, grief-stricken, then begs his brother to kill him and, by way of spurring on Paolo's anger, stabs Francesca. Paolo still refuses to raise a hand against his brother, and Lanciotto finally stabs him. As Malatesta and his attendants rush in, Paolo and Francesca fall to the floor and die in each other's arms. Lanciotto falls upon his brother's body, crying out to Malatesta:

> I killed thy son for honour: thou mayst chide.
> O God! I cannot cheat myself with words!

I loved him more than honour—more than life—
This man, my Paolo—this stark, bleeding corpse!
Here let me rest, till God awake us all!

(V, iii)

Francesca da Rimini is clearly superior to any American play written through the middle of the nineteenth century. Although it adheres to the general characteristics of the romantic tragedy of its day, Boker far surpassed his contemporaries in excellence of plotting, characterization, and dramatic verse.

There is relatively little overt action in the plot of the play, although it provides the conventional scenes of visual spectacle: processions, ceremonies, and groupings of supernumeraries. These are but accessory dressings, however, to the spare, tight structure of the central situation. Boker focuses intensely on his three major characters and allows them to play out their tragedy with a minimum of melodramatic plot contrivance. More than in any other play of its period, the characters of *Francesca da Rimini* determine the movement of the plot.

The figure of Lanciotto is deeply affecting. The critic William Winter described him most aptly:

A great soul, prisoned in a misshapen body, intense in every feeling, tinctured with bitterness, isolated by deformity, tender and magnanimous, but capable of frantic excess and terrible ferocity; a being marked out for wreck and ruin and bearing within himself the elements of tragedy and desolation.[13]

Lanciotto is a far cry from the jealous husband of conventional romance. His love for his brother is genuine and provides him with a motive force that conflicts with his own self-interest. His feelings about himself, about Francesca, and about Paolo are complex and ambivalent—constantly shifting and carrying him further into his unhappy involvement.

Francesca and Paolo too are drawn with complex feelings and attitudes—driven by passion but conscious of Lanciotto's unhappiness. Their scenes together are remarkably realistic and underscored with tension. Afraid of revealing themselves too fully, they mask their true feelings with deceptive courtesy, but the passion beneath the surface is made clear to us at all times.

Among the minor figures, Pepe the jester is utterly unique as a dramatic character. Although Boker had modeled him on the type of the court jester or "allowed fool" of Elizabethan comedy, Pepe exhibits as well qualities of the political malcontents, the melancholy cynics, and the Machiavellian villains of that earlier period. Pepe is Shakespeare's Feste, Touchstone, Thersites, Jaques, and Iago, all rolled into one.

Boker's rendering of blank verse in this play is masterful. The dialogue is almost totally free from the archaic diction, twisted syntax, and rhetorical bombast so typical of the American romantic play of the time. Boker's verse seems always appropriate to the speaker —elevated and eloquent in the case of the noble figures, easy and colloquial for Pepe and the humorous maidservant, Ritta.

Although it is never less than poetic, the play's dialogue reads at times like realistic, modern prose, making the play quite accessible to a modern reader. When the occasion demands, however, Boker proves himself an accomplished dramatic poet, as in the several excellent soliloquies assigned to Lanciotto. At times the unhappy hunchback reminds us of Hamlet:

> I am bemocked on all sides. My sad state
> Has given the licensed and unlicensed fool
> Charter to challenge me at every turn.

The jester's laughing bauble blunts my sword,
His gibes cut deeper than its fearful edge;
And I, a man, a soldier, and a prince,
Before this motley patchwork of a man,
Stand all appalled, as if he were a glass
Wherein I saw my own deformity.

(IV, i)

Strangely enough, *Francesca da Rimini* was not very successful when it first appeared in 1855. It is said to have been poorly acted at that time, although the critic of the New York *Daily Tribune* wrote of the opening performance: "The brilliancy of the first scene and the historical accuracy of the costumes and properties showed that the play had been conscientiously put upon the stage. . . . The play may be considered entirely successful."[14]

It was in its 1882 revival that Boker's tragedy gained the recognition it deserved. The actor Lawrence Barrett was responsible for this production and triumphed in it as Lanciotto. It opened at Philadelphia's Haverly's Theatre on September 14 and ran there for nine weeks —an unheard-of run for a poetic tragedy. When Barrett repeated the production nine years later, the distinguished critic and theater historian George C. D. Odell was in the audience and described the evening as "one of the most affecting performances I ever saw. . . . I was so moved, so exalted by the first visit to the play that I went immediately to see it again. . . . Credit to Boker and Barrett, high priests of the production."[15]

Still another notable production of *Francesca da Rimini* was that produced by Otis Skinner, who had played Paolo in Barrett's production, at Chicago's Grand Opera House on August 22, 1901. It subsequently enjoyed fifty-six performances in New York, as well as a road tour. Of Skinner's production, one anonymous critic wrote:

The sublime tragedy throws into pitiful contrast the mass of romantic trash that gluts the theatre today. How paltry and trivial seem the strutting mannikins of the machine made plays beside the loftiness and grandeur of this simple terrible tale. ... There is dignity in Mr. Boker's lines.[16]

Boker's only other play to be produced was *The Bankrupt* (Broadway Theatre, December 3, 1855), a prose melodrama in a contemporary setting that slipped away after four performances. Quinn and others identify it as the poorest of Boker's acted works for its stilted language, contrived plot, and indistinct characters.

George Henry Boker made a considerable impact upon the American theater in the 1850s and was widely recognized as a leading poet and dramatist of his time. From a modern perspective, however, it is the tragedy of *Francesca da Rimini* that renders Boker worthy of study. Had he written nothing but this single play, he would still be ranked among the major American dramatists.

7. DION BOUCICAULT: MASTER OF MELODRAMA

Some readers might question the inclusion of Dion Boucicault in a discussion of American dramatists, for Boucicault was Irish by birth and pursued his theatrical career in Ireland, England, France, and Australia, as well as in America. Nevertheless, Dion Boucicault must be reckoned with as one of the major figures in nineteenth-century American drama and theater. Actor, dramatist, producer, innovative manager, teacher—all these labels attach to the fascinating figure of Dion Boucicault, master of melodrama.

Boucicault turned out well over a hundred plays, many of which are now lost. Included in this prodigious output were some of the greatest popular successes in the history of the American theater, as well as some of its most dismal failures. Critical assessments of Boucicault's plays have varied. Some commentators have dismissed him as a purveyor of melodramatic claptrap—a master of sentiment and hokum—but others have found in at least a few of his better plays a craftsmanship that earns him a place among the best of the nineteenth-century dramatists, either English or American. All agree on one point at least: Dion

Boucicault knew how to please an audience and seldom failed in that assignment.

Boucicault's personal life was hardly less intriguing than the sensational melodramas with which he titillated his appreciative audiences. His birth and parentage remain even today a mystery, and it is generally thought that he was a child of adultery. At least five dates have been recorded for his birth: December 7, 26, and 27 of 1820, and December 20 and 26 of 1822. Of these, one of the 1820 dates is most likely. His father was either Samuel Smith Boursiquot, a Dublin wine merchant of French descent who was married to Dion's mother, or Dr. Dionysius Lardner, an encyclopedist with whom Dion's mother was known to have been romantically involved. It was Lardner who functioned most predominantly in the paternal role while the young boy was growing up—hence, the supposition of his adultery.

What little is known of Boucicault's boyhood and schooling comes from his own writings. By 1833, he tells us, he had moved to London. He was educated at various schools, including the College School of London University, a boys' grammar school. He never received a university education and was always, by his own admission, a poor student, full of high spirits and mischief. Nevertheless, he had a capacious intellect and schooled himself in literature and languages.

In 1837, Boucicault first set foot upon a stage, acting in a school play at Brentford. He was immediately, hopelessly, and permanently stagestruck. In the following year he took the stage name of Lee Moreton (a pseudonym he retained for a few years) and went to Gloucestershire to act professionally in provincial theaters. His London acting debut, as Lee Moreton, was in 1839.

Boucicault's playwriting career began in 1837, coincident with his acting career. His first play was *Na-*

poleon's Old Guard, revised and produced in 1842 as
The Old Guard. His first play to be acted was *A
Legend of the Devil's Dyke*, produced in Brighton in
October of 1838. Two more of his plays were pro-
duced professionally before his first great success,
London Assurance, appeared at Covent Garden on
March 4, 1841.

London Assurance, which brought Boucicault overnight fame, is one of his best plays. Frequently anthologized, it is said to represent a link between the
plays of Richard Brinsley Sheridan and those of Oscar
Wilde in the English comedy-of-manners tradition. It
is, in the words of Boucicault's recent biographer,
Robert Hogan, "almost the only notable comedy of
manners between the 1780s and the 1890s."[1]

The plot of *London Assurance* recalls the artificial
and conventional intrigues of Restoration comedy, but
its verbal sparring is a far cry from the elegant wit of
Congreve and his contemporaries. Boucicault's plot
features a typical love triangle between a dissipated
young rake, his ridiculous old roué of a father, and the
beautiful young heiress they both desire. Unfor-
nately, the movement of the plot depends upon the
youth's being mistaken by his own father for a stranger who just happens to resemble him in every detail
—a highly implausible contrivance.

Boucicault's dialogue in *London Assurance* consists
largely of pleasant banter rather than incisive wit, as
his cumbersome metaphors amply illustrate:

Etiquette is the pulse of society, by regulating
which the body politic is retained in health. I
consider myself one of the faculty in the art.
(Harcourt in Act I)

Love is a pleasant scape-goat for a little epidemic
madness. I must have been inoculated in my in-

fancy, for the infection passes over poor me in contempt.

(Grace Harkaway in Act II)

Although *London Assurance* attempts to make telling observations upon the artificiality of its society's obsession with fashion and etiquette, Boucicault's social commentary goes no deeper than, for example, the ladies' complaint that their exclusion from the gentlemen's after-dinner smoker is a "selfish, unfeeling fashion, and a gross insult to our sex" (Act IV).

The comedy's strength lies in its characterizations. Although the dramatist relied upon familiar types from the comedy of manners (the young rake, the aging lecher, the unfaithful wife, the fop, and so on), he endowed the people of *London Assurance* with individuality and good humor. Best of the characters is Lady Gay Spanker, Boucicault's original creation. Lady Gay is a bold and bouncy horsewoman who greatly enlivens the proceedings as she flirts with the old roué and scoffs at her milksop husband.

Audiences responded to *London Assurance* with great enthusiasm, although Edgar Allan Poe once termed it the "most inane and utterly despicable of all modern comedies."[2] Boucicault himself, never one to be deceived regarding his own artistry, admitted that the comedy "will not bear analysis as a literary production."[3] Nevertheless, *London Assurance* has much to please an audience. It was revived by the Royal Shakespeare Company in 1970 with considerable success. The production was brought to New York in 1974 and was well received.

In the five years following the brilliant success of *London Assurance*, Boucicault saw at least twenty more of his plays produced in London, assuring his position as an important new dramatist. It was in this period, too, that he first became a husband and, soon thereafter, a widower—all under mysterious circumstances befitting one of his own melodramas. He had married a French widow, probably in July of 1845, and moved with her to the Continent. One day they went mountain-climbing together in the Swiss Alps, but Boucicault came down alone. He gave out the story that his wife had fallen from the mountain, but the precise details of her death were never ascertained. He inherited £1,000 from the lady, however, and quickly spent it, ending up in Bankruptcy Court.

Sometime around 1850 Boucicault met, and presumably married, the English actress Agnes Robertson, with whom he was to live for nearly the remainder of his life. She bore him six children, and their marital status would never have come under question had Boucicault not, at the age of sixty-five, married still another actress, claiming that he had never wed Agnes Robertson. Whether Boucicault and Robertson were ever legally man and wife remains a mystery, but she was granted an English divorce from him after his third marriage, thus bestowing official legitimacy upon their children.

The years 1853 to 1860 were those of Boucicault's first American venture, during which he established himself in this country as a major theatrical figure, both as an actor and as a dramatist. He made his American acting debut in Boston in September of 1854 and his New York debut two months later as Sir Charles Coldstream in his own popular play, *Used Up*. In these years also he produced at least twenty-five plays in various American cities, including three that may be considered among his major dramatic works: *The Poor of New York*, *The Colleen Bawn*, and *The Octoroon* (discussed more fully at the close of this chapter).

The Poor of New York (Wallack's Theatre, December 8, 1857) serves as a perfect example of Boucicault's skill both in adapting French melodrama to American tastes and in further adapting and recoining his own work to accommodate whatever needs might arise. He fashioned his melodrama from a French play, *Les Pauvres de Paris*, by Brisebarre and Nus and it proved highly successful in New York. Consequently, over the years it appeared in other cities as, variously, *The Streets of New York*, *The Poor of Liverpool*, *The Streets of London*, *The Streets of Dublin*, *The Streets of Philadelphia*, and *The Money Panic of '57*. Boucicault had simply to change local place names and topical references, whatever the city.

In *The Poor of New York*, Boucicault established a successful formula for sensational melodrama—a formula that he was to use again and again. Included in this formula was the obligatory "sensation scene" that would provide for a spectacular staging effect and bring his hero or heroine to the brink of disaster, after which a rescue or escape would be effected. The sensation scene in *The Poor of New York* was the burning of a house; in subsequent Boucicault plays it took such forms as an underwater rescue (*The Colleen Bawn*), a blazing steamboat (*The Octoroon*), the perilous ascent of a prison tower (*Arrah-na-Pogue*), a boat race (*Formosa*), and a horse race that featured live horses (*Flying Scud*). These sensation scenes never failed to whip the Boucicault audience into a frenzy of excitement.

Boucicault had no illusions about literary art in the composition of these sensational melodramas. Writing after the success of *The Poor of New York*, he admitted: "I can spin out these rough-and-tumble dramas as a hen lays eggs. It's a degrading occupation, but more money has been made out of guano than out of poetry."[4] When *The Poor of New York* appeared in England as *The Streets of London*, one of its auditors was Charles Dickens, whose reaction nicely defines Boucicault's brand of melodrama: "It is the most depressing instance, without exception, of an utterly degrading and debasing theatrical taste that has ever come under my notice. For not only do the audiences—of all classes—go, but they are unquestionably delighted."[5] The audiences of New York most recently saw *The Streets of New York* in a musical adaptation in 1963.

The *Colleen Bawn; or, The Brides of Garryowen* represents the Boucicault melodrama pressed into the service of Celtic charm. It was the first of three highly successful Irish plays that Boucicault ultimately produced, the others being *Arrah-na-Pogue* (1864) and *The Shaughraun* (1874). *The Colleen Bawn*, adapted from Gerald Griffin's novel *The Collegians*, premiered at Laura Keene's Theatre in New York on March 29, 1860. Miss Keene, one of America's finest actresses, played the role of Anne Chute, an aristocratic young lady. Agnes Robertson was Eily O'Conner, the Colleen Bawn (fair-haired girl), and Boucicault himself triumphed in the featured role of Myles-na-Coppaleen, a roguish vagabond type that was to be recreated in the title role of *The Shaughraun*.

The Colleen Bawn, today the best known of Boucicault's Irish plays, was an enormous success. When it was acted later that year at London's Adelphi Theatre, it ran for 278 consecutive nights, a record run.

In addition to his plays, Boucicault made one other major contribution to American drama during his first American sojourn. He was instrumental in securing the passage of the Copyright Law of 1856. The previous law (1831) had proved totally ineffective in protecting American dramatists from piracy of their texts, unauthorized productions, and unscrupulous exploitation, such as that suffered by Robert Montgomery Bird at the hands of Edwin Forrest. Together with George Henry Boker, Boucicault succeeded in persuading Congress, in 1855, that a more comprehensive statute was needed. The resulting Copyright Law of 1856 went a long way toward protecting the rights of the dramatist, although it was far from perfect. It provided that an author possessed sole right to "print and publish," or to "act, perform, or represent" his play. Unfortunately, it called only for the registration of a play's title with the Library of Congress, rather than the deposit of the entire text, as is now the case. Still, Boucicault's contribution to the welfare of the American dramatist in this matter was considerable.

The years 1860 to 1872 saw Boucicault back in England and Ireland, acting, playwriting, and serving as manager and entrepreneur in a number of theatrical ventures. Two of the dramatist's plays from this period are worthy of note: *Arrah-na Pogue* and *Rip Van Winkle*.

Arrah-na-Pogue; or, The Wicklow Wedding premiered at the Theatre Royal, Dublin, on November 7, 1864, and was subsequently revised and played successfully in London. The second of Boucicault's major Irish plays, it earned the distinction of being translated into French by Eugène Nus as *Jean la Poste* and played in Paris for 140 nights. This Parisian success served as a response to those of Boucicault's detractors who had so often taken him to task for stealing from the French theater. Boucicault could at last claim that he had paid his debt. *Arrah-na-Pogue* also contained Boucicault's new lyrics to the old street ballad "The Wearing of the Green," a song that has since become virtually a national anthem for the Irish.

Boucicault's association with the great American actor Joseph Jefferson III was a long and fruitful one, and Jefferson acted in a number of the dramatist's plays. By far their most successful collaboration was a dramatization of Washington Irving's *Rip Van Winkle*, which they coauthored during Jefferson's

London visit in 1865. The work premiered at the Adelphi Theatre on September 4 of that year and proved to be the mainstay of Jefferson's subsequent acting career.

Jefferson had been playing another version of the Rip Van Winkle legend with minimal success, and it was Boucicault's expert theatrical sense that reshaped the work into a long-lived triumph. Jefferson freely admitted his gratitude for Boucicault's expertise, and the Jefferson–Boucicault version of *Rip Van Winkle* became a classic of the nineteenth-century American theater. Boucicault's recent biographer called the role of Rip "one of the great character roles of nineteenth-century theater."[6]

In 1872 Boucicault returned to America, formed a touring company, and spent the next couple of years writing and acting in such remote outposts as San Francisco and western Canada. It was in this period of his career that he wrote what may be the greatest of his successes, the Irish melodrama *The Shaughraun*. It opened at Wallack's Theatre on November 14, 1874, where it ran for 143 performances and grossed over $220,000. In London it scored a run of 119 performances. In all, Boucicault's profits from *The Shaughraun* have been estimated at over half a million dollars.

The Shaughraun follows the same formula for Hibernian melodrama that had brought Boucicault such success in *The Colleen Bawn* and *Arrah-na-Pogue*. It features two heroines, one a common peasant and the other a refined lady; its villainous landlord persecutes a helpless widow woman; its plot turns upon a misunderstanding; and it offers the obligatory sensation scene—in this case, a prison escape in which the scenery becomes a major performer:

> *The scene moves—pivots on a point at the back.*
> *The prison moves off and shows the exterior of*

tower, with CONN *clinging to the walls, and*
ROBERT *creeping through the orifice. The walls
of the yard appear to occupy three-fourths of the
stage.*

(II, v)

Spectacle notwithstanding, the real success of *The
Shaughraun* is its title character of Conn, the *shaughraun* ("wanderer" or "vagabond"), the role first
played by Boucicault himself. Conn is a youth of
about twenty who scampers through the plot like a
comic chorus figure—playing tricks, romancing, and
bringing off daring and heroic exploits. It is a tribute
to Boucicault's acting ability that he played the role
with full credibility while in his early fifties. It also is a
tribute to his physical stamina, for the role makes demands that would challenge an athlete:

Boucicault was perforce obliged to jump in and
out of cabin windows, to scale prison walls that
revolved in full view of the audience apparently
without human agency . . . to climb over abbey
ruins and execute a "back fall" down a precipitous
"run"; after being "stretched out" and "waked"
as a genuine corpse, to come to life for a hand-
to-hand encounter with a pair of ruffians; and
finally, from the inside of a barrel, shoot through
the bung-hole at the arch villain *Corry Kinchela*,
and afterward place the barrel over the colleen
Moya, thereby concealing her from view.[7]

The Shaughraun is not a great play by modern standards, but it is certainly one of the best of Boucicault's
crowd-pleasers. It is skillfully structured to provide its
implausible, sensational situations with a maximum of
credibility, and it contains several scenes of genuine
humor and Gaelic charm. The role of Conn is one of
the better acting parts of the period; the scene in
which he attends his own wake, commenting upon the

The Shaughraun. Cyril Cusack as Conn the *shaughraun* in the Abbey Theatre revival of 1967. Directed by Hugh Hunt; designed by Alan Barlow.

mourners, is brilliantly conceived. *The Shaughraun* proved its durability in a 1967 revival at Dublin's Abbey Theatre, with the fine Irish actor Cyril Cusack in the role of Conn. The Abbey production played in London as well, and both Irish and English audiences delighted in the Boucicault blarney as much as had their forebears nearly a hundred years earlier.

Boucicault's career as a dramatist declined after the success of *The Shaughraun*, although he continued to write plays and to act, making several trips between America and England from 1875 to 1885. In the latter year he was in San Francisco, where he produced what is generally considered to be his last play of any merit, *The Jilt* (California Theatre, May 13, 1885).

However one may assess Dion Boucicault as a literary figure, it cannot be denied that he was a major contributor to the American theater—to the theater as popular entertainment. He was the most prolific and most successful dramatist of his time. He was an actor of immense talent and popular appeal. And he was a producer-manager whose innovations altered the course of theatrical art in America.

Boucicault's work as a dramatist was at least ninety percent derivative. Most of his plays were either outright translations of previous dramas (usually from the French) or adaptations of earlier plays, stories, or novels. For this reason, he was frequently accused of plagiarism. By his own admission, however, originality was simply not among his major concerns in fashioning a successful entertainment. He once stated: "Originality, speaking by the card, is a quality that never existed. An author cannot exist without progenitors, any more than a child can. We are born of each other."[8] More important than originality to Boucicault was the reshaping of material to appeal to current tastes. And his strength as a dramatist lay in his uncanny talent for doing precisely that for well over forty years.

Boucicault once offered an appraisal of theatrical managers:

As a low state of health is liable to let in a score of maladies, so a low state of the drama has developed the *commercial manager*. This person in most instances received his education in a bar-room, possibly on the far side of the counter. The more respectable may have been gamblers. Few of them could compose a bill of the play where the spelling and grammar would not disgrace an urchin under ten years of age. . . . To the commercial manager we owe the introduction of the burlesque, opera bouffe, and the reign of buffoonery.[9]

His caustic commentary is ironic, for Boucicault was himself one of the most influential managers of his time. He did much to promote the drama by reducing the length of performances—by eliminating supplementary entertainments and featuring the play as the central attraction. He made popular the innovation of the box set in American theaters, employing it first in *London Assurance*. He instituted the tradition of the matinee, and he introduced fireproofing for scenery.

Most significantly, Boucicault's theatrical management contributed to the demise of the stock company, the form of theatrical organization that had obtained in America from the beginning. He was the first to form touring companies of a single play, rather than companies that toured with a full repertory. Thus, he promoted the play as the star attraction and deemphasized star actors.

Boucicault made and spent a fortune in his long and productive career, but he lived his final two years in near poverty, teaching acting for a meager salary and looking forward—always forward—to that next great hit, the one that never came. Dion Boucicault died in New York on September 18, 1890.

The Octoroon; or, Life in Louisiana

For the student of Americana, *The Octoroon* must surely rank as the outstanding Boucicault play. It is, in

The Octoroon. Engraving of the auction scene as performed at the Adelphi Theatre in 1861.

fact, among the best of all his dramatic works and perhaps the only one in which the dramatist utilized his set formula for domestic melodrama to explore honestly a real-life social problem—in this case, slavery. In *The Octoroon*, we find for once both the craftsman and the man of conscience surmounting the theatrical trickster.

Boucicault fashioned his plot from a novel by Mayne Reid, *The Quadroon*, although his reworking of the story is considerable. A secondary source was the contemporary novel *The Filibuster* by Albany Fonblanque, from which the dramatist took the plot device of the incriminating photograph. (Photography was still a novelty in 1859.)

The play opened at the Winter Garden Theatre in New York on December 5, 1859, with Joseph Jefferson playing Salem Scudder, Agnes Robertson as Zoe, the octoroon slave, and Boucicault in the minor role of the Indian Wahnotee, a pantomime part in which the actor made a powerful impression.

The play is set on the Louisiana plantation of Terrebonne, which is owned by Mrs. Peyton, widow of the late Judge Peyton, a generous man but a poor financial manager. Mrs. Peyton's nephew, George, returns to Terrebonne after a ten-year residence in Paris to learn that the plantation, mortgaged to the hilt, will be auctioned off unless Mrs. Peyton can obtain funds to prevent foreclosure on the mortgages.

One of the mortgagees is Jacob M'Closky, a villainous Yankee who had served as overseer for old Judge Peyton and had wheedled his way into control of the plantation. M'Closky is described by Salem Scudder, the "good" Yankee of the piece, as the "darndest thief that ever escaped a white jail to misrepresent the North to the South" (Act I). A second mortgagee is Mr. Sunnyside, a benevolent neighbor with a lovely daughter, Dora. Still another mortgage on Terrebonne is held by the New Orleans firm that is threatening foreclosure.

Dora Sunnyside arrives at Terrebonne to meet the returning George Peyton for the first time and promptly falls in love with him. George, however, has been smitten by his aunt's beautiful servant girl, Zoe, the illegitimate daughter of the late Judge Peyton. Mrs. Peyton treats Zoe like a daughter and assures George that "she has had the education of a lady." Scudder, too, is enamored of Zoe and tells George: "When she goes along, she just leaves a streak of love behind her. It's a good drink to see her come into the cotton fields—the niggers get fresh on the sight of her." George is therefore angered and puzzled by the offhand manner in which the other white people—especially M'Closky and Dora—treat Zoe. He does not yet know that the girl he loves is one-eighth black—an octoroon.

Zoe is desired also by the evil M'Closky, who is determined to take possession of both her and Terrebonne. He learns that a Liverpool brokerage firm, which owes the estate of Judge Peyton more than $50,000, has dispatched a check to Mrs. Peyton, due to arrive in the next mail shipment. He discovers as well that Zoe is still technically a slave, for the Judge had drawn up her free-papers while the plantation was encumbered by debt. Since Zoe, like all slaves, is property of the estate, the Judge could not legally free her. Thus, if M'Closky can possess Terrebonne, Zoe will be his. "I'll have her, if it costs me my life!" he snarls.

In the second act, George finally declares his love to Zoe, who reluctantly tells him the truth: "Of the blood that feeds my heart, one drop in eight is black." As an octoroon, she is forbidden by law from marrying him. Dora, meanwhile, has made no headway in her pursuit of George and asks Zoe to intervene in her behalf, pointing out that if George will marry her she will provide the money to save Terrebonne. Mrs. Peyton too pleads with George to propose to Dora, so that the plantation and its slaves will be saved from auction:

I do not speak for my own sake, nor for the loss of the estate, but for the poor people here: they will be sold, divided, and taken away—they have been born here. Heaven has denied me children; so all the strings of my heart have grown around and amongst them, like the fibres and roots of an old tree in its native earth. O, let all go, but save them!

(Act III)

George, moved by her eloquence, consents to court Dora. "I will sell myself," he nobly claims, "but the slaves shall be protected." When he attempts to propose to Dora, however, Zoe appears on the scene, and the love between George and Zoe becomes painfully obvious to Dora, who runs off weeping.

Meanwhile, Mrs. Peyton has dispatched one of her young slave boys, Paul, to the wharf to fetch the mail and, she hopes, the check from Liverpool that will save Terrebonne. Paul's constant companion is old Wahnotee, an Indian who speaks no English but is devoted to little Paul and treats him like a son. At the wharf, Paul and Wahnotee find Salem Scudder experimenting with his new hobby, photography. Scudder photographs Dora Sunnyside while Paul and Wahnotee look on. When Scudder, Dora, and Wahnotee leave, the impish Paul decides to take his own picture. He trips the time exposure shutter and runs to pose before the camera, seated squarely on the mailbag that contains the letter from Liverpool.

M'Closky skulks in, bent on intercepting the letter, and sees no alternative but to kill Paul, which he does with the tomahawk that Wahnotee left behind. M'Closky finds the letter in the mailbag and stands over Paul's body reading it while the photographic plate is still in the process of exposure. After he leaves, Wahnotee reenters and finds the body of Paul. The act ends with the old Indian smashing the camera and taking up the body of his beloved Paul as he wails in grief.

With the failure of the Liverpool letter to arrive, there is no hope for Terrebonne and the auction proceeds. In a scene of intense excitement and suspense, the land and buildings of the plantation are auctioned off, Mr. Sunnyside emerging as the victorious bidder, thanks to Dora's urging. The next items of property are the slaves, all of whom are auctioned off in quick order.

Zoe is the final item. Sunnyside, Scudder, and Dora all try to outbid the evil M'Closky, but M'Closky's determination to have the girl knows no limit, and he finally wins, bidding $25,000 as the price for his lust. It appears that evil has triumphed.

The fourth act takes place at the wharf, where the steamer *Magnolia* is about to sail. When Wahnotee arrives on the scene, M'Closky accuses the old Indian of the murder of Paul, citing the blood-stained tomahawk as evidence. The crowd rises up against Wahnotee and is calling for a lynching when Old Pete, an elderly slave, spots the photographic plate among the wreckage of the camera. The plate, which had captured the image of M'Closky standing over the body of the murdered boy with the purloined letter in his hand, makes M'Closky's guilt plain to all. A quick search of the villain produces the letter and check from Liverpool.

As M'Closky is being taken into custody, he bolts, grabs a torch from Old Pete, and escapes, flinging the torch into some leaky turpentine barrels. The wharf's shed catches fire, and the flames quickly spread to the *Magnolia*, which is then cut loose from her moorings. The act ends in a typical Boucicault "sensation scene." The blazing steamer moves off as M'Closky "*re-enters, swimming*" and makes his escape. But the final stage direction bodes ill for M'Closky: "Wahnotee *is seen swimming. He finds trail and follows* M'Closky. *The Steamer floats on at back, burning.*"

In the brief final act, Wahnotee overtakes M'Closky and pursues him off stage to what is presumably his death; we hear only M'Closky's off-stage screams. The heartbroken Zoe, unaware of the turn of fortune, comes to the slave quarters to obtain poison from Dido, a matronly slave woman. Having overheard George's declaration, after the auction, that he'd "rather see her dead than his [M'Closky's]," Zoe is determined to end her life. She returns to the parlor at Terrebonne, where she finds both Dora and George. She contrives to have George unknowingly administer the fatal potion to her and, in a heart-rending farewell scene, she bestows her blessing on the union of Dora and George, then collapses. Her dying words reveal her nobility of spirit: "I stood between your heart and hers. When I am dead she will not be jealous of your love for me; no laws will stand between us. . . . O! George, you may, without a blush, confess your love for the Octoroon." (For his London audiences, Boucicault altered the play's ending and allowed Zoe to live.)

In plot outline and structure, *The Octoroon* is not much different from scores of other Boucicault melodramas. The story combines a romantic intrigue with an economic calamity. A triangular love affair is complicated by a threatened mortgage foreclosure, and a black-hearted villain adds to the complications. A series of far-fetched incidents (for example, the incriminating photograph) keeps the story in motion. The characters speak in sentimental and emotion-charged hyperbole. There is the obligatory sensation scene.

Nevertheless, in *The Octoroon* Boucicault captured the mood and atmosphere of a specific time and a particular place. The play is redolent of antebellum Louisiana life; both its white and its black characters are presented with considerable realism. Dora Sunnyside, Salem Scudder, and Mrs. Peyton are quite sympathetic, and the several scenes with the "niggers" of Terrebonne offer an idealization of the slave–master relationship that is genuinely charming and frequently touching.

It is a tribute to Boucicault's genius that he managed in this play to present a fairly accurate, if idealized, picture of Southern plantation life and confront the problem of slavery without offending either the

North or the South. The villainous Yankee M'Closky is counterbalanced by the noble Yankee Scudder, just as the evils of slavery are mitigated by Mrs. Peyton's genuine devotion and protective concern for her slaves. One of the more moving scenes of the play finds Old Pete, the black patriarch, pleading with the other slaves to look their best at the auction, so that Mrs. Peyton will be proud of them. Southerners and Northerners alike praised Boucicault's play, even as the nation was on the brink of civil war.

It is ironic that one of the most topically "American" plays of the nineteenth century should have been penned by an Irishman, but Boucicault knew audiences—American, Irish, English, Canadian, or Australian—and could adapt his talents accordingly. A modern revival of *The Octoroon* at New York's Phoenix Theatre (January, 1961) earned kind words from the critics and captivated its audiences, who came to hiss the villain and cheer the hero but went away genuinely moved.

8. THE MOVE TOWARD REALISM

If there was any clearly discernible trend in the diversified American drama of the three decades following the Civil War, it was a movement away from the romanticism of the prewar years and toward realism. That is not to say, however, that the enthusiasm for romantic plays completely disappeared; the astounding success of Boker's *Francesca da Rimini*, for example, occurred in its 1882 revival. Nevertheless, American dramatists of the late 1860s, 1870s, and 1880s turned for the most part from the exotic settings and historical events favored by Payne, Bird, Boker, and their contemporaries. The postwar drama began to focus on American themes and characters and to depict recognizable settings from real life. Additionally, theatrical production styles altered to accommodate the shift; acting became more realistic, as did the scenery designed to dress the plays.

A number of important dramatists were at work in America during this period—too many for coverage here. Playwrights like Edward Harrigan (1845–1911) and Charles Hale Hoyt (1860–1900) wrote a new style of American comedy, one that focused upon contemporary life in middle- or lower-class characters. Harrigan, especially successful in depicting low life in the large Eastern cities, developed the ethnic stereotypes of the Negro, the Irishman, the German, and the Italian. He gave some three dozen plays to the stage, although some of them were little more than vaudeville sketches. Hoyt too depicted a wide range of recognizable characters, from clergymen to bartenders, from politicians to plumbers. Eighteen of his comedies were produced in the 1880s and 1890s.

Three of the leading literary figures of this period were Bret Harte (1839–1902), Mark Twain (1835–1910), and William Dean Howells (1837–1920); all three men were attracted to the theater and had varying degrees of success as dramatists. In the 1870s, Harte brought the realism of the West to the stage in two plays, one a collaboration with Twain, and he produced another drama in 1896 with considerable success.

Howells was the most prolific and successful of the three. He wrote some thirty-six plays, but most of them were one-acts and only half a dozen saw the stage. He specialized in realistic social comedies, satiric in tone and farcical in plot, that were concerned with the American aristocracy. Howells's settings were contemporary and recognizable, and his plays abound with topical references to current events, recent inventions, and real persons. He was unquestionably among the leaders in dramatic realism, but the one-act form was not attractive to producers. Had more of his works been acted, Howells's influence upon the American theater might have been considerable.

Although the decades under discussion saw the emergence of the professional American dramatist as an independent, creative artist, most of the plays produced were, like their forerunners, written by those who combined playwriting with other theatrical endeavors—principally production and management.

The present chapter focuses upon two major dramatists: Augustin Daly and Bronson Howard. Daly represents the tradition of the playwright-producer, while Howard was a dramatist exclusively. Both may be considered pioneers in the drama of realism. Furthermore, as a producer-manager, Daly was instrumental in bringing realism to the fields of acting and stage production, as well as to his own playwriting.

Augustin Daly (1838–1899)

The plays of Augustin Daly, some ninety in number, hardly appear to the modern reader as realistic, for they draw upon most of the melodramatic devices made popular by Dion Boucicault. Nevertheless, in his playwriting and in his production practices, Daly made important contributions to the rise of realism. He was called by Arthur Hobson Quinn the "first of the modern realists in American playwriting."[1]

Daly was born in Plymouth, North Carolina, on July 20, 1838. When his father, a sea captain and shipowner, died, Augustin's mother took the youth and his brother, Joseph Francis, to New York, where the boys frequented the theater. Even at an early age, Augustin Daly became fascinated with playwriting and production, although he never aspired to become an actor. Daly's career as a producer began with a boyhood experiment. At the age of eighteen, he staged a program of entertainments at the Brooklyn Museum, under the billing of "The Melville Troupe of Juvenile Comedians." The evening was something less than a success; the box office receipts totaled $11.25, while Daly was out $76.00 in expenses.

Despite this initial failure, Daly's success as a manager was rapid and substantial. He opened his first theater, the Fifth Avenue, in August of 1869 and produced twenty-one plays there within six months. In

January of 1873 he opened the nearby Daly's Fifth Avenue Theatre and assumed as well the management of the Grand Opera House and the Broadway Theatre for the season 1873–74. In the summer of 1875 he took his company on tour to Chicago, Salt Lake City, San Francisco, and other Western cities, bringing national recognition to the Daly company.

In September, 1879, Augustin Daly assumed control of the Broadway Theatre and transformed it into Daly's Theatre, a house that was to become the most popular in New York within four years. Daly's Theatre became known as the home of happy comedy, and Daly was acclaimed as the finest producer of Shakespeare and early English comedy. In all, he produced sixteen Shakespeare plays, some unfortunately mangled by "adaptation."

In addition to his productions of the classics and of his own plays, Augustin Daly was instrumental in encouraging the writing of new plays by other American authors. He produced some of Boucicault's works, and he launched the career of Bronson Howard by producing three of his first four plays. In addition, he encouraged playwriting from Bret Harte, Mark Twain, William Dean Howells, and Henry James—all with varying success.

Daly was the first to take a full American theater company to England and the Continent, and his several foreign tours earned him an international reputation for excellence in production. The European critics invariably remarked upon his company's uniquely realistic acting style. His first London tour was in 1884, followed by others in 1886, 1888, 1890, and 1891. Of one of the Daly company's 1886 performances, the *Saturday Review* wrote:

> There is not now in London an English company as well chosen, as well trained, as brilliant in the abilities of its individual members, or as

well harmonized as a whole, as the admirable
company which Mr. Daly directs. They suggest
the Comédie Française at its best.[2]

On the 1888 tour, Daly's production of *The Taming
of the Shrew* marked the first Shakespeare performance in Europe by an American troupe. In 1893,
Daly opened his own theater in London.

Daly's ensemble was the first complete American
company ever to play on the European continent. In
1886, their appearances in Hamburg and Berlin
brought English-language theater to Germany for the
first time in nearly three hundred years. They were
the first American company ever to perform in France,
although their reception by the Parisians was somewhat cool. Wherever the Daly company performed—
London, Berlin, Paris, or San Francisco—note was
always taken of their acting style, which largely did
away with the traditional declamatory delivery in
favor of a realistic, conversational tone.

Daly claimed authorship of about ninety plays in all,
including originals, translations, and adaptations. It is
known, however, that his brother Joseph Francis was
his constant collaborator and may, in fact, have been
the principal writer of most of their works. The two
brothers were very close, and Joseph Francis was content to have Augustin claim sole credit for their writing. Thus, we will never know precisely what portion
of the Daly plays are truly Augustin's.

The plays fall into three categories: originals,
dramatizations, and translations. The distinction is an
elusive one, however, for Daly, like Boucicault, felt
free to draw upon all available sources, and the term
"original" must be somewhat charitably applied. Nevertheless, some of Daly's works were distinctly original in that they derived from no single previous
source. Most of these were either sensational melo-

dramas of the Boucicault variety, or panoramic spectacles of metropolitan life that featured tableaux and
vaudeville-like entertainments. Only the melodramas
survive.

Daly's formula for melodrama was much like
Boucicault's, with the difference that Daly concentrated upon scenes of contemporary city life, depicting recognizable settings and drawing characters from
the metropolitan milieu. He wrote four of these, only
three of which survive: *Under the Gaslight* (1867), *A
Flash of Lightning* (1868), and *The Red Scarf* (1868).
All three are essentially commercial potboilers that
depend for their appeal upon a "sensation scene" in
the Boucicault tradition. In *Under the Gaslight* the
hero is tied to a railroad track while the evening express bears down upon him; *A Flash of Lightning* features a burning boat (as did Boucicault's *The Octoroon*); and the hero of *The Red Scarf* is bound to a
log that is about to be sawed in half in a burning
sawmill.

These plays were enormously successful. *A Flash of
Lightning*, for example, ran almost two months and
was subsequently played in a number of American and
English cities. One Daly commentator has pointed out,
however, that the play "combines the worst features
of *East Lynne* and *Uncle Tom's Cabin* in a melodramatic mélange that is improbable, frequently to the
point of sheer stupidity."[3]

The best and most enduring of the three is *Under
the Gaslight*, virtually an American classic because of
its "tied-to-the-railroad-tracks" climax. It opened at
the New York Theatre on August 12, 1867, and was
acted repeatedly in New York for twenty years. It
was produced in London in 1868, and it became a
staple of the American regional theater in cities like
Boston, Denver, Salt Lake City, and San Francisco.

Under the Gaslight, set in contemporary New

Under the Gaslight. The climactic railroad scene, as staged at Carnegie-Mellon University in 1972. Directed by Richard Shank; settings by Glenn Gauer; costumes by Carl O'Shea.

COURTESY OF CARNEGIE-MELLON UNIVERSITY DEPARTMENT OF DRAMA, PHOTO: WILLIAM NELSON

York, depicts such familiar scenes as Delmonico's, the Tombs Police Court, and Pier 30 on the North River. The unlikely plot concerns Pearl and Laura Courtland, supposed sisters and respected members of New York society. Laura is engaged to Ray Trafford, a wealthy socialite, but conceals a shameful secret: she is a foundling of unknown parentage.

Laura's engagement to Ray is disrupted by the appearance of Byke, a low-class villain who arrives to expose Laura's background and announce that he is her father. Society immediately rejects Laura and she moves from the Courtland mansion to set up housekeeping in a humble flat. Her only friends are

Snorkey, a one-armed Civil War veteran, and Peach-
blossom, a waif who was herself a victim of Byke's
machinations. The plot from that point forward concerns Laura's attempt to evade the evil Byke and his
woman, Old Judas, a slatternly type who claims to be
Laura's mother. Ray, meanwhile, turns his attentions
to Pearl and the two are to be married, although it is
obvious that he still loves Laura, despite her question-
able background.

The climactic scene occurs when Laura, who is
running from Byke, hides in a railway shed at Shrews-
bury Station, locked in for her own protection by a
kindly stationmaster. Snorkey, who intends to help
Laura, arrives at the station. Byke then appears, over-
powers Snorkey, and ties him to the railroad track. As
the train approaches, Laura peers helplessly from the
window of the shed in horror. She remembers a bun-
dle of axes that the stationmaster had earlier placed in
the shed and begins to chop her way through the
door. She rushes out to untie Snorkey just as the
"*locomotive lights glare on scene. . . . As* Laura *takes
his head from the track, the train of cars rushes past
with roar and whistle.*" Daly's staging of this scene
was said to surpass previous stage spectacles, and the
business was widely imitated in subsequent plays.

In the brief final act, Byke arrives at the Courtland
mansion intent upon robbing Pearl, but he is over-
powered by Ray and Snorkey. Byke, his villainy exposed, makes the surprising announcement that he and
Old Judas had exchanged Pearl and Laura as babies.
Thus, Pearl is the "beggar's child" and Laura is a blue
blood. This humbles the haughty Pearl and allows Ray
once again to turn to Laura. Word arrives that Old
Judas has conveniently fallen off a cliff and been
killed, so that Byke's threatened exposure of Pearl's
parentage will lack corroboration. Byke, his villainy
foiled, makes a hasty departure, and Laura and Ray

turn bravely toward "tomorrow," which will "bring the long sought sunlight of our lives."

Under the Gaslight is a curious blend of realism and implausible contrivance. Much of the dialogue is quite natural-sounding, especially the street slang and comic banter of Snorkey and his cohorts. Snorkey is virtually a character out of naturalism. Despite the loss of his right arm in the service of his country, he remains a patriot. "I promised Uncle Sam I'd stick to the flag— though they tore my arm off, and by darnation I stuck!" he tells Laura. "I stood up to be shot at for thirteen dollars a month" (II, i). Snorkey and the other figures of New York's lowlife give the play a fairly realistic tone.

Nevertheless, the plot of *Under the Gaslight* is artificial and unbelievable, dependent upon such melodramatic ingredients as kidnaping, child abuse, a chloroforming, a near drowning, concealed identities, and startling eleventh-hour revelations. The "babies-switched-at-birth" device is the sort of silly stuff so deftly satirized by Gilbert and Sullivan, and Byke's unmitigated nastiness places him as the conventional villain of third-rate melodrama. One wonders if it was in reference to *Under the Gaslight* that J. R. Towse observed of Daly's work: "Some of the pieces that he produced were unmitigated trash, flagrant melodramatic absurdities, with no other possible object than to catch the mob."[4]

The best of Daly's original plays is *Horizon*, a satiric melodrama of the American frontier. It opened at the Olympic Theatre on March 21, 1871, and enjoyed a seven-week run. *Horizon* is a flawed but intriguing work that combines the most improbable and contrived plot devices with highly realistic dialogue and sharp character portrayals. In it, Daly accurately captures the romance of the legendary West.

Horizon's plot is too silly to be recited in detail, as

an account of its principal ingredients will show: a New York society matron whose dissipated husband kidnaped their only daughter years earlier and took her to live on the "horizon" of the American West; a land-grabbing congressman who obtains a deed to a large chunk of the Western Territories but is unable to take it from the grubby squatters who occupy it; two love affairs, one a vexing triangle involving the long-lost heiress; a large contingent of Indians who mount two full-scale attacks upon the palefaces; a chorus of darkies who literally "tote that barge" and "lift that bale"; a brave Irish widow and her dizzy daughter; a town drunk; a card shark; an Indian papoose who clings to the paleface hero; a panorama of a boat trip downriver (like Dunlap's *A Trip to Niagara*, forty years before); and an eleventh-hour rescue of the white women from the Indians by a band of government soldiers.

This unlikely collection of plot materials is assembled by Daly with not much dramaturgical skill but with delicious humor. One senses a playwright enjoying himself and pulling the collective leg of his gullible audience. *Horizon* perpetuates the myth of the American frontier that we all know and love, tinting its unlikely complications in the rosy glow of romanticism. It provides a clear indication of Daly's sense of humor and his keen ear for realistic speech.

The bulk of Daly's dramatic works were translations of foreign plays and dramatizations of popular fiction. He dramatized ten novels in all, most of which were recent works with psychological insights and domestic themes. (His feeling for realism was obvious even in his choice of source material.) Among the more successful of these dramatizations was *A Legend of Norwood* (1867), from Henry Ward Beecher's novel; two plays from Dickens's works, *The Pickwick Papers* (1868) and *Oliver Twist* (1874); a treatment of *L'Assommoir* (1879) by Emile Zola, himself a strong advocate of realism; and *Divorce* (1871), based upon Anthony Trollope's *He Knew He Was Right*. The latter was especially successful, opening at the Fifth Avenue Theatre on September 5, 1871, and running for 236 performances, the longest run of any comedy in the New York theater at that time. *Divorce* had a long stage history throughout the country and was at one point playing simultaneously in five major cities.

Like William Dunlap more than half a century before him, Daly was responsible for bringing the current French and German stage successes to American audiences. Daly's translations are the plays most tenuously linked to his authorship; he knew neither French nor German and relied upon literal translations in the preparation of his English texts. Moreover, he is known to have provided only the scenarios for most of these translations, leaving the writing of the dialogue to his brother, Joseph Francis. Nevertheless, history records Augustin Daly as the author of these pieces.

Daly produced forty-two plays from the German theater, claiming authorship of thirty-six of them. One of the more successful was the first play he ever produced, *Leah the Forsaken*, adapted from *Deborah* by S. H. von Mosenthal. It opened in Boston on December 8, 1862, and was subsequently staged in New York and in London with considerable success. Daly's German translations were quite popular, and from 1875 on, German farces were a staple of every Daly season.

Daly's productions of French plays were not so popular, and only two of his translations ran for more than a hundred performances. Nevertheless, he produced sixty-five plays from the French, forty-four of which he claimed as his own. Thus, in his thirty-five-year career as producer, he offered an average of two

French plays per season. His favorite sources were Sardou and Dumas, but his best and most successful French adaptation was *The Lottery of Love* (October 9, 1888), from *Les Surprises du Divorce* by Bisson and Mars. This comedy capitalized upon the current issue of women's suffrage and ridiculed the contemporary fashion of women's bloomers.

Augustin Daly was a major theatrical figure of his time. As a producer he advanced the cause of realism in staging techniques and in acting. His several foreign tours did much to bring international recognition to the American theater. As a dramatist his contributions are perhaps less certain, since the bulk of his plays were derivative. Nonetheless, his staging of classic plays and of current European dramas enriched the American theater. He once stated: "It does not matter whether an American dramatist chooses American material or not. His work, so long as it is added to the volume of work done in America and in the American spirit, belongs to the American drama."[5] Augustin Daly died in Paris on June 7, 1899.

Bronson Howard (1842–1908)

"Dean of the American drama," "America's first professional playwright"—these are the labels that have traditionally attached to the name of Bronson Howard, author of the distinctive Civil War drama *Shenandoah* (1888). Although Howard was certainly not the first American to write plays professionally, he was the first who devoted his career exclusively to playwriting, serving neither as actor, like Payne and Boucicault, nor as producer, like Dunlap and Daly. Bronson Howard must be credited with establishing playwriting in America as a legitimate and lucrative profession. He gave seventeen plays to the American theater, a number of which enjoyed considerable success.

Howard was born in Detroit, Michigan, on October 7, 1842, the son of Charles Howard, a merchant who became mayor of Detroit in 1849. Young Bronson went to Connecticut in 1858 for schooling that would prepare him to enter Yale, but he gave up his college plans in favor of a career in journalism. He wrote for the Detroit *Free Press*, and his first play, *Fantine*, was produced in that city in 1864. He was to continue his journalistic activities until 1876, well after his career as a dramatist had been launched.

Howard moved to New York in 1865 and worked for the *Tribune* while Horace Greeley was its editor and for the *Evening Post* under William Cullen Bryant. He became seriously interested in writing for the theater at this time, and his first New York play, *Saratoga*, opened at Daly's Fifth Avenue Theatre on December 21, 1870. *Saratoga*, a satiric comedy of life in a resort town, ran for 101 nights and showed Howard's facility with realistic comedy. It was a great success in England as well, after a few minor rewrites and a title change to *Brighton*.

Howard's next two plays were, like *Saratoga*, produced by Daly. *Diamonds*, a comedy of manners set in New York and Staten Island, opened in September of 1872, and *Moorcroft*, a rather poor melodrama, was unsuccessfully performed two years later. Neither is of particular interest, but Howard's next play, *The Banker's Daughter*, is. This comedy went through three stages of development—an evolution that is carefully chronicled in Howard's *Autobiography of a Play*, an 1886 lecture that was subsequently published (1914). Howard gives a detailed account of his working method in changing an earlier play, *Lillian's Last Love* (1873), into *The Banker's Daughter* (1878) and finally into *The Old Love and the New* (1879), the title under which it played in London. Howard's interesting account of the play's metamorphoses is proof of his care and craftsmanship in playwriting.

Howard's style of playwriting changed significantly in 1882 with the appearance of *Young Mrs. Winthrop* (Madison Square Theatre, October 9), his first major social drama. His ten previous plays had been either light farces or melodramas, but *Young Mrs. Winthrop* signaled a shift to fairly realistic examinations of contemporary society. The play depicts the failure of an upper-class marriage due to the wife's preoccupation with social convention and to the husband's neglect of his home for his business affairs. Howard mixed comic and serious material in the play but omitted the satiric thrust typical of his earlier comedies. In the characters of Douglas and Constance Winthrop, Howard found the type of well-to-do socialites upon whom he was subsequently to focus almost exclusively.

Howard's use of the American business world as dramatic material was most successfully realized in *The Henrietta* (Union Square Theatre, September 26, 1887), a domestic melodrama set in the world of Wall Street wheeling and dealing. It is perhaps his finest realistic play and one that is strikingly modern in its attention to ticker tapes, telephones, and electric lights.

The Henrietta concerns the Vanalstyne family of New York, headed by Nicholas Vanalstyne, a millionaire speculator and the Giant of Wall Street. Vanalstyne has a daughter, Mary, and two sons, Nicholas, Jr., and Bertie. The former son emulates his father's financial wizardry in a fiercely competitive and unscrupulous drive for power and wealth, while Bertie is an aimless but pleasant youth of no noticeable ambition.

The senior Vanalstyne, a widower, wishes to marry Cornelia Opdyke, a widow, but he is so preoccupied

with his investments and his ticker-tape machine that
he can't behave like a feeling human being. In the
midst of his proposal to her, the stock indicator begins
ticking and he abandons the lady for the machine.
Vanalstyne, Jr., is even less of a human being; although married, he has fathered a child by a lower-
class woman and abandoned her and the child. Moreover, we learn that he is secretly speculating against
his father's interests in the Henrietta Mining and Land
Company and is determined utterly to ruin his father
and emerge as the new Giant of Wall Street. The
mother of the junior Vanalstyne's illegitimate child
dies, but not before sending a packet of incriminating
letters to his wife, Rose, at the Vanalstyne home.
Nick, Jr., succeeds in creating the impression that the
culprit in the affair is not himself but his brother Bertie. Bertie, out of consideration for his brother's marriage and his affection for Rose, accedes to the false
charge, thus ruining his own hopes for marriage to
Agnes, Rose's younger sister.

The seriousness of the main plot is alleviated by a
considerable amount of comic foolery involving a
misunderstanding over the name Henrietta, which
comes to mean different things to different characters.
Henrietta is, of course, the name of the stock in which
the Vanalstynes are speculating, but it is also the name
of a racehorse upon which Bertie and Vanalstyne's
new son-in-law, Lord Arthur Trelawney, intend to
place bets. And to the ladies, Henrietta is an actress of
ill repute in whom their menfolk seem dangerously
interested. This confusion is but one of several farcical
touches in the plot that prevent *The Henrietta* from
bogging down in the bathos of domestic melodrama.

The plot reaches its crisis in the third act, when
Vanalstyne, Jr., has succeeded in driving the Henrietta
stock so low that he has ruined his father; but the
action is suddenly reversed when the ingenuous Bertie

invests his inheritance of half a million dollars to drive the Henrietta stock back up and save Vanalstyne, Sr. This occurs in a scene of intense excitement as the ticker-tape machine spells out the fate of the Vanalstynes and the hands of the clock move toward the market closing hour. Vanalstyne, Jr., defeated at last, suffers a heart attack and dies, unfortunately taking with him the truth of his profligacy and of Bertie's innocence.

The final act, however, effects a happy resolution to all this distress—a resolution marred, unfortunately, by much artificial contrivance. The incriminating packet of letters, thought to have been burned at the end of Act II but in reality saved from the fire by Mrs. Opdyke, is revealed to Rose, who realizes that her husband was a faithless two-timer and that Bertie has been deeply wronged. Thus, Bertie and Agnes are allowed to marry; Rose gives her hand to the family physician, who has loved her for years; Vanalstyne finally wins the hand of Mrs. Opdyke; and the play closes on a tableau of three happy couples, accompanied by the music of "The Wedding March."

In *The Henrietta* Howard treats big business as the distinctively American subject for drama; his thesis is that preoccupation with finance is destructive of the happy conduct of human affairs. Greed prompts Vanalstyne, Jr., to the ruin of his own father and the slander of his brother, just as it stands in the way of the senior Vanalstyne's romance with Mrs. Opdyke. Vanalstyne is basically a good man who loves his family, but he is also one who can chuckle with glee at having ruined his "dearest old schoolmate" in the market. Business becomes the instrument of fate in determining the life or death of those who indulge themselves in it. It kills Vanalstyne, Jr., just as Dr. Wainwright predicts that it will in the first act:

You New York business men have invited Death
into your own houses. The telephone and the
stock indicator have enabled His Sable Majesty
to move up town with the rest of the fashionable
world; he used to content himself with wearing
out your souls and bodies at your offices. . . . You
are doing what hundreds of young men are doing
in this city today: Wearing your life out in the
greatest gambling hell on earth. There is death
in the street.

Howard's realistic treatment of big business among
New York's upper class appealed greatly to his audiences. *The Henrietta* ran for sixty-eight weeks and
made half a million dollars. In 1913 it was revived in
New York as *The New Henrietta*.

Bronson Howard's other major success, and the play
for which he is best known today, was *Shenandoah*, a
sprawling, epic drama of the American Civil War.
The play was first staged in Boston in November of
1888, where it failed. Fortunately, the producer
Charles Frohman saw the work and was convinced
that it was salvageable. He suggested some alterations
to Howard and the playwright complied. When the
revised *Shenandoah* opened at New York's Star Theatre on September 9, 1889, it was an instant and colos-
sal success. It ran for 250 performances in its initial
staging and remained a major attraction on American
stages for the next fifteen years.

Shenandoah encompasses the entire Civil War, focusing upon a number of fictional characters whose
lives and loves are affected by it. The first act opens at
Charleston Harbor on the eve of the firing on Fort
Sumter, and the final act occurs after the surrenders of
General Lee and General Johnston, which marked the
close of the four-year conflict. The plot of the drama
is complex and filled with incident, involving a number of character relationships.

Central to the play are two pairs of lovers, separated and kept apart by the vicissitudes of war. Kerchival West, a Union colonel, and Robert Ellingham, a colonel from Virginia, have been close friends for years and were classmates at West Point. As the firing upon Sumter commences, they become unwilling enemies fighting on opposite sides of the conflict. West loves and is loved by Ellingham's sister, Gertrude, while Ellingham is similarly involved with Madeline, West's sister. Each girl is, therefore, the political enemy of the man she loves.

An important subplot involves a misunderstanding between West and General Haverhill, his commander. Haverhill suspects that his wife is romantically involved with West, but it is the villainous Captain Thornton of the Secret Service who, enamored of Mrs. Haverhill, is promoting the General's suspicion in an attempt to discredit West. An additional complication involves General Haverhill's son, Frank, a fugitive from the law whom the General has disowned out of shame. Frank arrives at the scene of battle, in disguise, to fight in his father's regiment and regain his good name. The General fails to recognize his own son, who has grown a beard and taken a false name, and he dispatches the boy on a dangerous mission, during which he is killed.

Still another subplot concerns the romance of Jenny Buckthorn, daughter of a Union major-general, with one Captain Heartsease, whom we are led to believe has died in battle but whom the dramatist happily resurrects at the play's finale.

These multiple entanglements become quite complex as the play progresses, but the final act offers a happy resolution. Before the final curtain falls, General Haverhill is apprised of Thornton's plot against Mrs. Haverhill's and West's reputations, thanks to a letter written by young Frank just before his death.

Thus, Haverhill and his wife are happily reconciled and become the guardians of Frank's widow and young son. Ellingham and Madeline are at last united, and West, who, like Heartsease, had been presumed killed, suddenly appears in good health to announce that he and Gertrude are married. Jenny and Heartsease are to be wed, and the play closes on a scene of marital bliss strikingly similar to that of *The Henrietta*'s final moment.

The great appeal of *Shenandoah* undoubtedly lay in its theatricality, its opportunities for spectacle, and its easy sentiment and patriotism, rather than in any intrinsic merit as drama, for the work is seriously flawed. It offers an excess of incident and a diffusion of focus that are epic rather than dramatic. So many major characters are involved that none is treated with any depth, and the reader or spectator is easily confused as to who is in love with whom and which character is on which side of the war. The confusion is more acute, of course, on the page than on the stage.

Additionally, Howard has employed a great deal of artificial plot contrivance in *Shenandoah* that is only minimally plausible and is aimed more at theatrical effect than dramatic probability. Frank's deathbed dictation of the very letter that will prove Thornton's villainy and West's innocence is contrived only to provide a last-act deus ex machina, and it is accompanied by an incriminating miniature of Mrs. Haverhill, mistakenly thought by her husband to be a love token but actually a deliberate red herring planted by Thornton. All this, as well as the sudden reappearance of characters we have supposed dead, is the stuff of third-rate melodrama.

Finally, there is little by way of characterization in *Shenandoah* to involve a reader or spectator. This is due principally to Howard's employment of easy sentiment and "knee jerk" patriotism, which renders the drama's figures bland, sentimental, and even maudlin in their expressions of emotion. In *Shenandoah*, friendship is saccharine and romance is as fragile and "sensible" as the worst examples of eighteenth-century sentimental comedy.

Shenandoah nevertheless provides many opportunities for grand moments on stage: music and marching, military displays, live horses, and a spectacular "retreat from battle" scene at the close of Act III. As the wounded and bedraggled Union troops are about to surrender, General Sheridan rides upon the scene and, accompanied by the encouraging shouts of Gertrude, spurs the men on to a counterattack and victory. This scene continues the tradition of battle scenes in American patriotic dramas first seen in Burk's *Bunker-Hill* (1797).

The reason for *Shenandoah*'s great success was probably most succinctly expressed in its New York *Times* review, written by Edward A. Dithmar:

> Mr. Howard has painted his new picture of American life on a very large canvas. It is crowded with figures. In the background the bloody contest for the preservation of the Union is waging. . . . The author has spared no effort to emphasize the sentimental idea of the brotherhood of the contesting parties in our terrible war, and the recognition by individuals on either side of the natural ties which bound them to their foes.[6]

In addition to promoting realism in the American theater through his own plays, Bronson Howard did much to enhance the reputation and welfare of American dramatists in general. In 1891 he founded the American Dramatists Club, a union of playwrights intended to promote professionalism and artistic security for its members. This group became the Society of American Dramatists and Composers, the forerunner of the present-day Dramatists' Guild. Through the Dramatists Club, Howard was able to effect the reform in copyright laws that made play piracy a misdemeanor punishable by imprisonment. It was the final step in the legal protection of the American dramatist.

Howard insisted always that the drama should be wed not to literature but to the art of the theater. His first test for the worth of a drama was always its viability on the stage. He once wrote to Brander Matthews:

> I think the divorce [of the drama from literature] should be made absolute and final; that the Drama should no more be wedded to literature, on one hand, than it is to the art of painting on the other, or to music or mechanical science. . . . I have felt this so strongly, at times, as to warmly deny that I was a "literary man," insisting on being a "dramatist."[7]

Bronson Howard died at Avon, New Jersey, on August 4, 1908. In his own playwriting, in his struggles on behalf of his colleagues, and in his conviction that the drama was an independent art form, Howard earned the labels of "Dean of the American drama" and "America's first professional playwright." His contribution to the American theater was succinctly expressed by Richard Moody:

> By his own example and by his persistent crusading, Howard brought new recognition and honor to American playwrights. He had no vested interest in theatrical production as manager or actor. He was not a refugee from the world of belles-lettres, venturing a casual and apologetic fling at dramatic writing. He was a professional playwright, moderate, careful, and committed to learning and practicing his art.[8]

9. REALISM ACHIEVED

As the century drew to a close, the profession of dramatist was well established in the American theater, and the number of successful American playwrights was considerable. Most of those whose names are known today were notable as practitioners of stage realism, but they did not reform the American theater overnight. The process of change was slow, as audiences did not easily relinquish their fondness for mindless melodrama and frivolous farce. Then, as now, people went to the theater primarily to be entertained, not to think.

Nevertheless, the final two decades of the nineteenth century saw the establishment of realism as a viable mode for playwriting, acting, and stage production in the American theater. Among the more successful dramatists of the period were such writers as William Gillette (1855–1937), the actor-dramatist whose play *Sherlock Holmes*, based on Conan Doyle's detective character, became a classic of the American stage; Augustus Thomas (1857–1934), a prolific dramatist from the Middle West whose works reflect native life and the love of country; Clyde Fitch (1865–1909), who excelled in social comedy and was to become perhaps the most popular playwright in the first decade of the new century; and two writers whose works illustrate the establishment of realism in acting, stage production, and playwriting: David Belasco and James A. Herne.

Belasco and Herne began their theatrical careers at approximately the same time. They were, in fact, co-workers in their early days in San Francisco during the 1870s. Both were directors as well as dramatists, and Herne enjoyed as well a stellar career as an actor. With the best works of Belasco and Herne, realism may be said finally to have prevailed in the American theater.

David Belasco (1853–1931)

It is difficult to know where or how to place David Belasco in a discussion of American dramatists. His playwriting career spanned more than sixty years—from his first effort at the age of twelve to his final adaptation in 1928. He represents, therefore, several decades in the development of American drama. Furthermore, his fame as a producer and director often overshadowed his accomplishments as a dramatist, despite the staggering number of plays that bear his name as author. Finally, the Belasco canon is so permeated with rewrites, adaptations, and collaborations that it is impossible to cite a precise figure in numbering his works. One fact is clear, however: the career of David Belasco cannot be omitted from a discussion of the rise of realism in American drama.

Belasco was born in San Francisco on July 25, 1853, and the first three decades of his life were spent in the American West. Young David was hopelessly stage-struck, and the theatrical experiences of his formative years were many and varied. He appeared frequently on stages in and around San Francisco, until his family moved to Victoria in 1858, following the dream of instant wealth that lured so many in the Gold Rush years. In Victoria, the boy appeared as the young Duke of York in Charles Kean's production of *Richard III*.

The Belasco family returned to San Francisco in 1865, after which David was privileged to work with some of the leading figures in American theater. He played a bit part in Augustin Daly's *Under the Gaslight* in 1869. In 1873 he served as secretary to Dion Boucicault in Virginia City, Nevada, where he developed an admiration for Boucicault's brand of sensational melodrama that is clearly evident in many of Belasco's early plays. From Boucicault, Belasco learned the meaning of "theatrical." Still another valuable association was that with James A. Herne, which began in 1874. Belasco eventually became Herne's prompter and stage manager at the Baldwin Academy of Music in San Francisco.

During these early years in and around San Francisco, David Belasco accumulated a formidable set of theatrical credentials. By age eighteen he had written at least a dozen plays. By age twenty-nine he had acted more than 170 roles, had written over 100 plays (including rewrites and adaptations), and had directed or supervised the staging of roughly 300 productions. When he moved to New York in 1882, he had already enjoyed a career that, for others, might have represented a lifetime of work in the theater.

Belasco's arrival in New York marked a decided advance in his career. His first Broadway play, *La Belle Russe* (Wallack's Theatre, May 8, 1882), was a solid success and was subsequently produced in London in 1886. It was the first of 123 Broadway productions with which he was to become involved during the remainder of his life. In that same year he became stage manager at the Madison Square Theatre, directing the premiere of Bronson Howard's *Young Mrs. Winthrop*, the success of which is discussed in the preceding chapter.

From 1886 to 1890, Belasco was stage manager for the Lyceum Theatre. In these years also he formed a playwriting partnership with Henry C. De Mille (1850–1893), a collaboration that secured his reputation as an important new American dramatist. Together Belasco and De Mille produced four plays, all directed by Belasco with considerable success. *The Wife* (1887), *Lord Chumley* (1888), *The Charity Ball* (1889), and *Men and Women* (1890) are all social dramas of contemporary life in New York that attest to Belasco's interest in realistic subject matter.[1] Although they may strike the modern reader as dated and melodramatic, they were acclaimed for their naturalistic dialogue and for Belasco's realistic approach to the creation of stage environment.

The year 1895 marked another advance in Belasco's career. With the production of his Civil War drama, *The Heart of Maryland* (Herald Square Theatre, October 22, 1895), he became an independent producer and thereafter turned his attention as much to the realistic reform of stagecraft as to playwriting. *The Heart of Maryland*, one of Belasco's major successes as both playwright and director, bears some resemblance to Bronson Howard's *Shenandoah*, produced six years earlier.

As in Howard's play, Belasco's subject is the conflicting loyalties suffered by characters caught in the midst of the struggle. The hero is Colonel Alan Kendrick of the Northern forces, son of Hugh Kendrick, a general in the Confederate Army. Thus, father and son find themselves military enemies, despite their familial bond. The setting is, as the title suggests, Maryland, but Maryland is also the name of the heroine of the piece. It is in and around the home of Maryland Calvert that the play's intrigue plot of spying and treachery unfolds.

Maryland loves Alan, even though he is an enemy to the South. Through the machinations of a villainous spy, Colonel Thorpe, Alan is wrongly accused of betraying military secrets, is captured by the Confederate forces, and is faced with execution at the hands of his own father, General Kendrick, who must place honor and duty above paternal love. Maryland too is torn between her love for Alan and her duty to the South, but she cannot stand by and see him executed, so she aids his escape.

The climactic scene of the drama occurs when Alan —who, with Maryland's help, has escaped imprisonment within the old church—is threatened with recapture if the Sexton rings the tower bell, a prearranged alarm signal. As the villainous Thorpe shouts orders for the ringing of the bell, Maryland scrambles up the tower and *"leaps and clings with both hands to the tongue of the bell. The bell moves higher and higher; she is dragged backwards and forwards by the swing. Shouting, etc., kept up until the curtain falls."*

This "sensation scene" in the Boucicault tradition threw the drama's audiences into paroxysms of excitement, thanks mainly to Belasco's realistic staging. It accounted largely for the play's enormous success with its audiences (and for the contempt with which the critics greeted the work). *The Heart of Maryland* ran for 229 consecutive performances, confirming Belasco's reputation as New York's leading playwright-producer. It subsequently toured the United States, and the American company played the work in London in 1898, an unusual recognition of the prestige of Belasco's ensemble.

After *The Heart of Maryland*, the character of Belasco's playwriting began to change; his penchant for sensational and thrilling spectacle gave way to a taste for more refined and subtle concepts of stage action that emphasized mood, atmosphere, and character emotions. The best of Belasco's plays were written after this date, and among the best are the three that he wrote with his second major collaborator, John Luther Long (1861–1927).

Belasco and Long coauthored three highly successful plays, all of which were produced and directed by Belasco. Best known of the three, through its operatic adaptation, is *Madame Butterfly* (Herald Square Theatre, March 5, 1900), based upon Long's earlier story of a Japanese girl who is wed and subsequently deserted by an American naval officer. (The operatic version, *Madama Butterfly*, was composed by Giacomo Puccini and produced in New York in February, 1907, with the great tenor Enrico Caruso as the naval officer, B. F. Pinkerton. The work has become a favorite in the operatic repertoire, although few remember the Belasco–Long original.) The other two plays by Belasco and Long were *Darling of the Gods* (Belasco Theatre, December 3, 1902) and *Adrea* (Belasco Theatre, January 11, 1905). The former, a tale of love and adventure set in Japan, was enormously successful, running for two years and receiving subsequent productions in London, Berlin, Italy, and Australia. *Adrea*, possibly the best of the three, is a romantic tragedy of ancient Rome whose heroine is a blind princess. Arthur Hobson Quinn wrote of the three Belasco–Long collaborations as plays that represent

romance which scorns restriction, which has the high courage that soars beyond the provincial, to deal with universal passions and emotions, which rides right at the five-barred gate of probability, knowing that if it fails, it falls into the ditch of nonsense, but if it rises triumphant, it outlines against the sky the imperishable figures of literature.[2]

In the thirty-year segment of his career that belongs to the twentieth century, David Belasco earned a degree of fame as a producer and director that overshadowed his reputation as a playwright. As a director, he brought to America the European tradition of the *régisseur*—a tradition well established on the Continent as early as the 1870s by directors such as the Duke of Saxe-Meiningen, André Antoine, and Constantin Stanislavsky.

Belasco the director was absolute dictator over every aspect of production—script, scenery, acting, lighting, music, properties, and so on—all in the service of a literal and detailed realism that was often overwhelming. For each of his productions he kept a detailed promptbook that meticulously outlined every moment in the progress of the play. In the apologia of his theatrical career, *The Theatre Through Its Stage Door* (1919), he explained his devotion to, and reverence for, stage realism:

> If, as I conceive it, the purpose of the theatre be to hold the mirror up to nature, I know of no better place to obtain the effects of nature than to go to nature itself. To fulfil this purpose with integrity, to surround the mimic life of the characters in drama with the natural aspects of life . . . is, I contend, the real art, the true art of the theatre. He who goes direct to nature for the effects he introduces on the stage can never be wrong, because nature itself is never wrong. It is upon this creed that I base my faith in realism in dramatic art.[3]

Belasco carried his realistic revolution into the purview of stage scenery by doing away with the traditional scenic flat (painted canvas over a wooden frame), often building real rooms on his stage. He insisted that every element of the setting not only *appear* real but *be* real. For his production of *Du Barry* (1901) he imported antique furniture and drapes of the Louis XV period. For *The Governor's Lady* (1912) he reproduced a Childs' Restaurant on stage, with the famed Childs' pancakes being cooked during the action. For *Tiger Rose* (1917) the floor of his stage forest was strewn with dried pine needles, and the audience marveled at the scent that wafted across the footlights, completing the environment of the Canadian Northwest.

In stage lighting, too, Belasco was a pioneer and an innovator. As early as 1879 in San Francisco he had experimented with the elimination of footlights and the use of spotlights from the front of the balcony railing as his primary light source. He was the first to conceive of stage light as a means of creating mood and atmosphere, rather than a mere source of general illumination. He pioneered the use of color media to negate the flattening effect of stark white light. In *The Wife*, he utilized a soft light and a glowing fireplace to underscore the privacy and intimacy of a marital discussion. The critics remarked upon the effectiveness of the technique.

The fame of Belasco's lighting effects has, in many cases, outlived the fame of the plays in which they occurred. No critic of the drama would seriously contend that either his *Madame Butterfly* or his *Rose of the Rancho* (1906) is a great play, but theater historians still chronicle his achievements in lighting these productions. For *Madame Butterfly*, Belasco created a fourteen-minute lighting effect that depicted the passage of night and the coming of the dawn as Cho-Cho-San stood silhouetted against the *shoji* screens, awaiting the arrival of her beloved Pinkerton.

And in his immensely popular *Rose of the Rancho* (359 consecutive performances), Belasco enthralled audiences and critics alike by creating, through lighting, the searing heat of the California desert.

Perhaps the best example of David Belasco's achievement in stage realism was his melodrama *The Girl of the Golden West* (Belasco Theatre, November 14, 1905), set in the era of the California Gold Rush. It ran for three years and, like *Madame Butterfly*, achieved lasting fame in an operatic version by Puccini, *La Fanciulla del West* (1910).

The "Girl" of the title is Minnie, proprietress of the ramshackle Polka Saloon in the Sierras. The Polka serves as home to miners, gamblers, Indians, and an assortment of colorful characters (remembered, the playwright claimed, from his youth). Minnie falls in love with Dick Johnson, who is really the outlaw Ramerrez but a "good guy" nonetheless. Johnson is hunted by Jack Rance, the quasi-villainous gambler-sheriff of the piece.

The highpoint of the play occurs in the second act, when Rance has tracked Johnson to Minnie's mountain cabin. Minnie hides her lover, who is wounded and bleeding, in the loft. When Rance confronts her, she denies knowing of Johnson's whereabouts. As Rance turns to leave, a drop of blood falls from the loft onto his hand, and he knows that his quarry is trapped. Seizing upon Rance's passion for gambling, Minnie persuades him to play a game of poker—the stakes to be Johnson's freedom if she wins, her person if she loses. As a blizzard rages outside, the suspenseful poker game is played out, and Minnie wins, albeit by cheating. Johnson is safe and Rance, true to his word, leaves the cabin.

After the climactic scene of the dripping blood and the card game, the remainder is anticlimactic. Johnson is captured by the miners but Minnie once again saves

The Girl of the Golden West. The villainous Jack Rance (*right*) challenges the poker players at the Polka Saloon. From the American Conservatory Theatre (San Francisco) 1979 production, directed by Edward Hastings.
PHOTO: WILLIAM GANSLEN

him and the two go off into the California sunrise to a new and better life in the East.

In staging this utterly implausible yet somehow endearing fluff, Belasco created a mise-en-scène that became the wonder of American theatergoers for years. His scenic prologue is among the legends of theatrical history. His curtain rose upon a distant view of the mountain at whose foot the Polka Saloon was situated. Then, through the use of rolling panoramas, cutout drops, and lighting, the spectator "traveled" down the mountainside as the saloon seemed to move nearer, until finally the stage was fully occupied by the interior of the saloon, the setting of the first act. This prologue was a coup de théâtre seldom since equaled and one that anticipated the "pan down" technique in filmmaking. Of course, the use of panoramas and dioramas on the stage was nothing new. It was, in fact, a technical throwback to the earlier theater (for example, Dunlap's *A Trip to Niagara*, 1828). But Belasco was able to imbue such standard scenic devices with an astounding degree of realism and create illusions of great persuasiveness.

The Girl of the Golden West offered at least two other scenic highlights: the second-act blizzard outside Minnie's cabin and the desert sunrise effect that accompanied the play's epilogue. The realism of Belasco's snowstorm was a major technical achievement. The blizzard was seen to cover the landscape, to ice the windows, and to send wisps of snow into the room through the chinks in the walls, as the wind howled portentously outside. This storm was, in reality, the concerted effort of thirty-two carefully rehearsed stagehands, performing a variety of backstage chores under the direction of a master technician who "orchestrated" their work. (In 1905, stagehands came cheap.)

The Sierra Nevada sunrise of the drama's epilogue remains today one of Belasco's more famous stage-lighting effects. According to his own account, he experimented with the effect for three months and spent five thousand dollars on that one brief moment—all to send Minnie and Dick Johnson happily off to their future in the East. Such tireless experimentation and reckless expenditures were typical of David Belasco's approach to stagecraft.

It is likely that Belasco's infatuation with scenic and lighting effects—with the technical and mechanical aspects of production—prevented him from fully realizing his potential as a dramatist. His best writing was done in collaboration with others, and none of his plays, despite their phenomenal success with their audiences, endures today as a notable example of dramatic art. Yet his feel for the dramatic and his keen ear for realistic speech are evident in the best of his work, among which one must place *The Return of Peter Grimm* (Belasco Theatre, October 17, 1911).

This play represents possibly Belasco's finest work as a dramatist. It is a highly realistic drama nearly free of melodramatic effects or sensational theatricalism, in which the writer dealt with a subject that profoundly interested him: the possibility of the dead returning to communicate with the living. His interest in the subject led him to approach his task with a degree of artistry that transcends his other dramas. If there is a Belasco play that might engage theatergoers today, it is surely *The Return of Peter Grimm*.[4]

The title figure of the drama is an elderly Dutch horticulturist who has built a successful tulip business with the dream of leaving it to his nephew, Frederick, whom he expects to wed his ward, Catherine. Grimm is essentially well-meaning but obtusely insensitive both to Frederick's opportunism and to Catherine's obvious affection for another man, James Hartman, Grimm's secretary. We soon learn that Grimm is, unknowingly, terminally ill, and he dies at the end of the first act—but not before extracting a sacred promise from Catherine that she will wed Frederick within ten days.

The second act opens with Catherine's dilemma at having to honor her guardian's dying wish and marry Frederick when it is James she loves and is loved by in return. Her anguish is compounded by Frederick, who drops his pious pose after his uncle's death and reveals himself for the greedy, heartless cad the others knew him to be all along.

The family physician, Dr. MacPherson, a believer in psychic phenomena, had earlier persuaded Peter Grimm into a half-joking agreement that whichever

The Return of Peter Grimm. A scene from Belasco's original 1911 staging, showing the meticulous detail of stage setting. David Warfield (*right*) as Grimm.

of them died first would attempt to come back—to return to the other and try to make contact. And true to his word, in the middle of the second act Peter Grimm, or his spirit, reappears. But he is invisible and inaudible to all on stage.

What Grimm's return makes painfully clear to him is that he had erred in his faith in Frederick and his insistence that Catherine wed him. His task, therefore, is to make known to the living his disapproval of Frederick and his desire to release Catherine from her promise. In order to communicate these feelings, Grimm requires a medium, and his medium is found in the character of little William, a child who is very ill and is being cared for in the Grimm home. William is also, it turns out, the illegitimate child of the profligate Frederick.

We realize that William is able first to sense and eventually to see Grimm's spirit because he himself is close to death. In the opening act, Grimm had promised to take the boy to the circus, and a Clown had appeared at Grimm's window to sing to the boy. Throughout William's subsequent scenes, the Clown's music recurs, heard only by Grimm and the boy, to underscore William's impending demise.

Through William, Grimm is able eventually to communicate his feelings about Frederick and Catherine to them and to the others. Frederick's duplicity and paternity are exposed; Catherine and James are happily united; and the play ends with the death of little William, who is led off by Grimm to eternal peace and the happiness that is death.

The Return of Peter Grimm, which ran for 231 consecutive performances, was one of Belasco's major successes, and deservedly so. It represents the epitome of his career as a playwright. Its supernatural subject matter, far from being exploited in a sensational fashion, is handled with sensitivity and a high degree of realism. Its characters are entirely plausible. Frederick is no mere stage villain but a wrong-headed young man who is capable of conscience and regrets. Grimm himself is beautifully drawn—good-humored, devoted to his home and family, but obstinate and myopic in his determination to meddle in the lives of the young people. His deep friendship with Dr. MacPherson is convincingly presented, with humor and realistic banter, in a surprisingly brief period of time.

There is sentiment in the play, but it is sentiment honestly expressed, with restraint and an avoidance of the excessive emotionalism so typical of the time. The deaths of Grimm and William convey a sense of affirmation and wonder, as does all the spiritualism that pervades the plot. In short, Belasco avoided the pitfalls inherent in his thesis and presented a drama of human emotions with honesty and sensitivity. *The Return of Peter Grimm* is well worth the attention of the modern reader.

David Belasco had more than his share of detractors. His enormous popular success led constantly to accusations of his pandering to poor taste, and he was frequently dismissed as a mere technician or a theatrical trickster. Yet Belasco himself admitted that his aim was primarily to please and that he considered the making of plays a craft rather than an art.

He had no use for the "drama of discussion" made popular by Ibsen and his followers; social and ethical issues held no great interest for him. His concern was for human situations, feelings, and the expression of emotions. Like Bronson Howard, he insisted that the drama should be separated from the field of literature and he made his contempt for the "literary drama" plainly known:

> The literary drama is very beautiful—for the library shelves. . . . It lives, of course—on the library shelves. But it is not actable, because it does not get beneath the vest. So I am not literary, because my target is the emotions. . . . The province of literature is entirely outside the province of the theatre.[5]

He maintained that the judgment of drama required standards different from those applied to literature and that his own plays were written to be acted, not to be read.

Belasco shunned the term "dramatist," preferring instead the label of "playwright," a distinction that had a real significance for him. "A wright is a workman," he once wrote.

We say wheelwright, shipwright . . . why not playwright? A wright takes the materials he finds to his hand and builds or forms them into coherent shape. He makes nothing; he only puts together more or less deftly. The materials he works with are scattered around. He takes them, chips them, varnishes them, fits them into place, and so erects his structure.[6]

Within this definition, David Belasco was a master playwright.

Belasco was active as a producer almost until the last. In 1921 he was honored as the foremost director in the United States at a dinner given by the Society of American Dramatists and Composers and the Society of Arts and Sciences. He produced his last play, an adaption of Molnar's *The Red Mill*, at his own theater in December of 1928, at the age of seventy-five. David Belasco died in New York on May 15, 1931.

James A. Herne (1839–1901)

James A. Herne's recent biographer, John Perry, titled his study of the actor-dramatist *James A. Herne: The American Ibsen*.[7] The comparison is most apt, for Herne's influence upon the course of the American drama—as actor, director, and playwright— was as decisive as the Norwegian writer's was in changing the course of European drama. The plays of James A. Herne may be said to mark the point at which mindless melodramas and frivolous farces began to take a back seat to dramatic realism in America, paving the way for the major dramatists of the twentieth century.

James A'Herne (the A at some point became a middle initial) was born of Irish stock on February 1, 1839, in Cohoes, New York. His father was an irascible tyrant and boozer with, ironically, a puritanical contempt for the theater and for actors. When James was thirteen he sneaked away to Albany with his brother to see Edwin Forrest act, and from that day forward his fate was sealed. Herne later wrote that he was so impressed with Forrest's performance that he "cast all former ambitions to the wind, and resolved to be an actor." His admiration for Forrest's art remained powerful throughout his life.

The young Herne began his professional acting career at the Adelphi Theatre in Troy at age twenty. This debut soon led to other engagements in Albany, Washington, Baltimore, and finally the newly completed Ford's Theatre, where he remained in the company for three years. His impressive talent was quickly recognized, and he gained much respect both as an actor and as a person from all who knew him. His fellow actor Nat C. Goodwin wrote of the young Herne: "In his early days he was prone to much dissipation, even to ruffianism; but he always drank and fought before the world. He was honest even when violently inclined. . . . And even in those days everybody loved the man."[8]

By 1864 Herne was playing Shakespeare at Philadelphia's Walnut Street Theatre, and in 1866 he acted at the Theatre Royal in Montreal, where he met the actress Helen Western, who became his wife for a brief time. Herne joined the company headed by Western and her sister Lucille, and their touring brought the actor to San Francisco for the first time in 1868. It was upon his return to that city in 1874 that James Herne the actor became James Herne the dramatist as well.

Herne's first play was *Charles O'Malley, The Irish Dragoon*, written for Tom Maguire's New Theater, where he served as stage manager (director). The text of the play has not survived. Two years later, Maguire made him stage manager of the new and opulent Baldwin Academy of Music, in which capacity he first met the Irish actress Katharine Corcoran, accepted her into the company, and subsequently fell in love with her.

Herne and Corcoran (known to all as K.C.) were married in 1878—an example of marital bliss that is probably unequaled in the annals of the theater. Although Herne was seventeen years her senior, they shared a happy marriage and a productive artistic life. K.C. was his leading lady, his constant critic, and the inspiration behind his creative efforts. Their daughter later described her mother as the "spark that was needed to light up the fires of genius that were smoldering in father's soul." Herne wrote most of his leading female roles expressly for his actress wife; she was the original Margaret Fleming.

It was in San Francisco also that Herne began his association with David Belasco. Herne hired Belasco as his assistant-prompter, and during the year 1879 the two collaborated on a number of projects, including the writing of plays. They first coauthored *Within an Inch of His Life*, a trashy melodrama fashioned from a French novel. This was followed by *Marriage by Moonlight*, *The Millionaire's Daughter*, and other similarly insignificant crowd-pleasers. The pair caused quite a sensation when they coproduced *The Passion*, a religious spectacle that established Belasco's reputation as a virtual wizard with stagecraft and nearly got the two men jailed for supposed sacrilege. The Christ of their passion play was, incidentally, James O'Neill, matinee idol and future father of Eugene O'Neill.

Herne's most important collaboration with Belasco in his San Francisco days was the play *Chums* (Baldwin Theatre, September 9, 1879), a sentimental domestic melodrama set on the Massachusetts seacoast. *Chums* gave early evidence of Herne's penchant for stage realism, both through his characterizations of the simple folk it portrayed and through some scenes of remarkably naturalistic dialogue. The play also reflected Herne's love for the New England seacoast and its people—the setting and character types upon which he was to draw for most of his plays.

Chums offered considerable realism in its staging as well as in its writing, and the San Francisco *Chronicle* review of September 14 remarked upon "some of the most realistic scenery ever seen upon a stage." The play's staging included a live cat that stretched itself and drank milk on cue (Belasco's wizardry), the consumption of a full dinner of real food by the dramatis personae, and an adorable baby that gurgled and cooed—also on cue.

Although *Chums* played only two weeks in San Francisco, Herne and Belasco took the play to Chicago and New York, under the new title of *Hearts of Oak*, by which name it is known today. After a slow start and some critical discouragement, *Hearts of Oak* caught on with the public and remained in Herne's repertory for years. The New York *Times* (March 30, 1880) called the play a "dull, long-winded, ultra-sentimental drama of a kind long deceased, and, we had hoped, not liable to resurrection." But such criticism failed to deter the public, and *Hearts of Oak* eventually netted Herne over $100,000.

Herne's next play was *The Minute Men of 1774–75* (Philadelphia's Chestnut Street Theatre, April 6, 1886), a historical drama with, according to John Perry, a "claptrap plot, flat characters, and cornball theme."⁹ It was followed by *Drifting Apart* (People's Theatre, May 7, 1888), a temperance drama that broke new ground, taking American playwriting away from the formula melodramas of the Boucicault variety. *Drifting Apart* offered realistic portrayals of human characters caught up in distressing problems—problems for which there are no easy solutions.

Herne had no regard for conventional melodrama,

believing that it failed to confront the truth of the human condition and offered instead only mindless entertainment. Thus, *Drifting Apart*, in its uncompromising realism, was a far cry from the typical nineteenth-century temperance play, such as *The Drunkard* or *Ten Nights in a Bar Room* (both 1850). Of melodrama, Herne once wrote:

> Seriously, melodrama is valueless to the progress of dramatic art. Seen under the analytical microscope, it is false to almost every aspect and color of life, and eternally comic to the judicious, in its absurdities of perspective and proportion, its grotesqueries of calcium and characterization. Like crimps and crinoline, or the difficult stock tie of our periwig-pated grand parents, the melodrama has outlived its day of usefulness.[10]

Herne was eventually to express his convictions on the nature of dramatic truth in an article titled "Art for Truth's Sake in the Drama" (1896), in which he stated:

> It is generally held that the province of the drama is to amuse. I claim that it has a higher purpose— that its mission is to interest and to instruct. It should not *preach* objectively, but it should teach subjectively; and so I stand for truth in the drama, because it is elemental, it gets to the bottom of a question. It strikes at unequal standards and unjust systems.[11]

Thus, "Art for Truth's Sake" became the Herne dictum—the guiding principle of his dramatic writing and of his acting technique.

In no Herne play is "Art for Truth's Sake" more potently embodied than in *Margaret Fleming*, possibly his most important contribution to the American drama. So uncompromising was this play in its approach to the subject of marital infidelity and the double standard that no producer would touch it, and Herne was forced to produce the play himself. Thus, *Margaret Fleming* opened in a modest production in Lynn, Massachusetts, on July 4, 1890.

In order to provide the work a broader hearing, Herne produced *Margaret Fleming* again nearly a year later in Boston. Still unable to find a backer and a major theater for the play, he rented Chickering Hall, a small recital hall, and converted it into a little theater. This performance of *Margaret Fleming* (May 4, 1891) has been called the beginning of the Free Theatre movement in America, and Herne has been likened to André Antoine, founder of the French Théâtre Libre.

The story line of *Margaret Fleming* is quite simple. The setting is Canton, Massachusetts, where Philip Fleming, a mill owner, and his wife, Margaret, reside. The Flemings enjoy what appears to be an ideal marriage, and their union has recently been blessed with a baby girl. We quickly learn, however, that Philip has committed an indiscretion and has fathered another child by a woman named Lena. The only person who knows that Philip is the father of Lena's child is Philip's doctor, a self-righteous moralist who appears with the news that the unfortunate Lena is dying and takes Philip to task for abandoning the girl.

As an added complication, the Doctor discovers that Margaret is suffering from glaucoma and might lose her eyesight entirely if she suffers any shock. Thus, she must not learn of Philip's infidelity. But Fate intervenes. The dying Lena is, coincidentally, the sister of Margaret's German nurse, Maria. Thus, Margaret learns of the dying girl and her fatherless child and goes to aid the poor woman.

Margaret arrives too late. Lena has died, but not before penning a note addressed to Philip that makes clear his paternity of her child. Margaret reads the note, realizes that the child is his, and, in shock and desperation, sends for her husband. The third act closes with a pantomime scene in which Margaret, alone on the stage, takes up the crying child and comforts it. As she moves about the room, she stumbles over a chair and we realize that she is going blind. Philip enters, but she does not see him:

> *Philip stands in dumb amazement watching her. The child begins to fret her again. She seems hopeless of comforting it. Then scarcely conscious of what she is doing, suddenly with an impatient, swift movement she unbuttons her dress to give nourishment to the child, when the picture fades away into darkness.*

The final act is devoted to a discussion between Philip, who returns after having run away for a week, and the blind Margaret, who is now caring for both of his children. She informs him that she can never again love him as a wife. He vows, nevertheless, to remain with her in the hope that he can one day earn her respect and win her back. Upon this inconclusive note the play ends. (The present text of the play presents a revision of Herne's original ending, in which Philip turned to alcohol, Margaret's blindness was pronounced permanent, and the two separated—a more artistically satisfying denouement, albeit a tragic one.)

In outline, *Margaret Fleming* displays an obvious resemblance to Ibsen's *A Doll's House* (1879); there is more than a suggestion of Ibsen's Nora in Margaret as she surveys the wreckage of her marriage. "Ah, Philip," she cries, "the old Margaret is dead. The truth killed her." The chief difference between the two plays is that the marital breakup between Nora and Torvald is brought about not by infidelity but by Nora's realization that their marriage is a sham. Herne, on the other hand, is concerned with the issue of the double standard. When, in the last-act discussion, Philip sullenly berates himself for his infidelity, Margaret calmly replies: "Oh, you are a man—people will soon forget." When he is unable to comprehend her refusal ever to sleep with him again, she responds: "Can't you understand? Philip! . . . Suppose—I—had been unfaithful to you?" He is shocked and repelled by the suggestion, and she pursues her point: "There! You see! You are a man, and you have your ideals of—the—sanctity—of—the thing you love. Well, I am a woman—and perhaps—I, too, have the same ideals."

American audiences of 1890 were not prepared for this frank discussion of marital infidelity, nor could they tolerate Herne's disregard for their cherished illusions about the sanctity of marriage. Moreover, Herne's style was too realistic. There were no grand moments of passion, no soliloquies, no surprising reversals of fortune—no features, in other words, of conventional domestic melodrama. Herne's audiences were shocked particularly by Margaret's nursing scene; the critics lashed out at the "sordidness" of Herne's vision with nearly the same viciousness with which they had attacked Ibsen when he created *Ghosts* (1881).

Margaret Fleming did not reach New York until seventeen months after its original performance in Lynn. It opened at Palmer's Theatre on December 9, 1891, and did very poorly there. The New York press was especially hostile. Typical of the reviews that greeted Herne's work was that by Edward A. Dithmar in the *Times* (December 10), which read in part:

> *Margaret Fleming* is, indeed, the quintessence of the commonplace. Its language is the colloquial English of the shops and the streets and the kitchen fire-place. Its personages are the every-day non-

entities that some folks like to forget when they go to the theatre. It is constructed in defiance of the laws of Aristotle and Horatius Flaccus and Corneille and Hazlitt. . . . The life it portrays is sordid and mean, and its effect upon a sensitive mind is depressing. . . . The stage would be a stupid and useless thing if such plays as *Margaret Fleming* were to prevail.[12]

The popular press notwithstanding, more enlightened commentators upon American letters found considerable merit in *Margaret Fleming*. Those who advocated, or at least recognized, the trend toward realism in both European and American drama were especially complimentary. William Dean Howells, possibly the most respected writer of the time, wrote to Herne that the play "has the same searching moral vitality as Ibsen's best work, and it is most powerfully dramatic."[13] Howells also defended the production in an article in *Harper's* magazine:

The power of this story, as presented in Mr. Herne's every-day phrase, and in the naked simplicity of Mrs. Herne's acting of the wife's part, was terrific. It clutched the heart. It was common; it was pitilessly plain; it was ugly; but it was true, and it was irresistible.[14]

Margaret Fleming was the pivotal work in Herne's career as a dramatist, and a turning point in the whole course of American drama. Its significance has been succinctly expressed by Perry:

It forced critics to revise archaic standards of criticism, brought realism to the American stage, inspired playwrights to write more intelligent native works, and proved that "little" theatres worked in practice. Finally, it created interest in an independent American theatre association.[15]

If *Margaret Fleming* proved unpalatable to both the public and the critics, Herne's next major play proved the exact opposite. *Shore Acres* became the most famous and best loved of his plays. The work premiered in Chicago (McVicker's Theatre, May 23, 1892) to a receptive press but closed after three weeks. Herne then took it to the Boston Museum, where it broke all Museum records, running for 113 performances. In 1893 it opened in New York (Fifth Avenue Theatre, October 30) to rave reviews and again broke records in its long run. It remained in Herne's repertory for five years and made him a millionaire.

Shore Acres is a domestic comedy-melodrama set on the coast of Maine, on Frenchman's Bay. It is rich in local color, realistic detail, and sharp, believable characterizations. The plot concerns Martin Berry, owner of Shore Acres Farm and keeper of the Berry Lighthouse. His large family includes a wife of unquestioning patience, Ann; several small children; a strong-willed, freethinking daughter, Helen; and his older brother, Nathaniel, called Uncle Nat. The latter is the central character of the play—a kind, goodhearted, folksy sage and veteran of the Civil War.

Against the wishes of Uncle Nat, Martin decides to mortgage Shore Acres and engage in some land speculation by subdividing the farm into residential lots, by way of capitalizing on an expected building boom. The brothers also disagree when Helen falls in love with Sam Warren, a young physician who is an evolutionist and an agnostic. Martin cannot abide the young man and forbids him to see Helen, despite Uncle Nat's defense of the young couple. Sam decides to move West and establish himself, with the hope of returning later to marry Helen. A misunderstanding arises in which it is believed that Sam has stolen one hundred dollars from the local storekeeper to finance his trip west. Martin Berry threatens to shoot the young man, which provokes a violent argument with Helen. Thus, Helen decides to run away with Sam, with Uncle Nat's approval and aid.

The couple make their flight on a fishing boat, the *Liddy Ann*, as a storm begins to rage. In the third act, set inside the lighthouse, Uncle Nat is about to light the beacon that will guide the *Liddy Ann* around the treacherous rocks during the storm, but Martin intervenes, claiming he would rather see his daughter dead than married to Sam Warren. The two brothers quarrel violently. Uncle Nat throws Martin to the floor and, near exhaustion, struggles up the long, steep steps to light the beacon. A scenic display next shows the exterior of the lighthouse and the imperiled boat. The glow of Uncle Nat's lantern is seen to move up from window to window as he ascends the stairway within. The scene ends as the beacon blazes forth, saving the boat and the young lovers.

In the final act, fifteen months later, winter has settled upon the farmhouse; it is Christmas eve. Martin has not spoken a word to Uncle Nat since their fight, but he has mortgaged the farm and subdivided it for the expected building boom. Word arrives that the Land Company has gone bankrupt; Martin is ruined and will lose the farm. This unhappy news is tempered somewhat by the unexpected return of Helen and Sam with their new baby. Ashamed of his foolish past behavior and affected by the sight of his first grandson (whom the parents have wisely named Martin), Martin has a change of heart, is reconciled to his brother and his daughter, and accepts Sam as his son-in-law. At that point, a letter for Uncle Nat arrives from the United States Government, informing him that he is to receive a large veteran's pension—one large enough to pay off the mortgage on the farm. All ends happily, the family goes off to bed, and the play ends with

Uncle Nat alone on stage, as he closes up the house for the night, beaming benevolently all the while.

The reader of *Shore Acres* is struck immediately by Herne's extensive and detailed stage directions. The play seems, indeed, almost an outline for an exercise in stage realism rather than a drama in the literary sense. The second act, for example, is given over almost entirely to the preparation and consumption of an entire home-cooked turkey dinner. Almost nothing occurs during the scene to advance the plot; the spectator's attention is directed to the details of the cuisine. The dialogue that accompanies this business is of a sort that might have been heard in a real Maine kitchen in 1890 —colloquial, homely, and trivial. Such domestic realism, a novelty in 1892, was a decided treat to Herne's audiences, but it can hardly engage a playgoer in the 1980s.

The realistic tone of *Shore Acres* is violated in only two instances, both of which, Herne admitted, were concessions to audiences accustomed to conventional melodrama. The first is the lighthouse sequence, reminiscent of a Boucicault "sensation scene," with Uncle Nat bravely climbing the steps to light the beacon as the *Liddy Ann* moves perilously closer and closer to the rocks. This business was a crowd-pleaser, but the entire scene could be cut from the play with no damage done to the narrative. Equally melodramatic is the last-minute "rescue by pension," a deus ex machina that Herne deplored but consented to in order to provide a happy ending and appease the producers.

One of *Shore Acres'* finest moments can only dimly be appreciated by a reader: the closing pantomime sequence in which Uncle Nat (Herne himself) closes up the house for the night. All the critics took note of the affective power of this revolutionary, five-minute sequence of silence, and modern commentators have noted that the scene strongly suggests the closing moments of Chekhov's *The Cherry Orchard*, a play that was to appear twelve years later. Again, Herne was ahead of his time. Of the effect of this scene, and of Herne's acting of it, the editor B. O. Flower wrote:

> During the four times I saw "Shore Acres" performed, the audience seemed rapt until Uncle Nat disappeared. It was one of the most remarkable illustrations of the unconscious tribute paid by the people to the genius of the artist and his fidelity to truth that I have ever seen.[16]

There is no question that the success of *Shore Acres* was due largely to the character of Uncle Nat and to Herne's performance in the role. The character descends from the stage-Yankee tradition that dates back to Jonathan in Tyler's *The Contrast* (1787), but Uncle Nat is a fully developed and affecting (albeit overly sentimental) characterization, not a comic caricature like Tyler's Jonathan. The role was the highlight of Herne's acting career—a career that easily places James A. Herne among the greatest of American actors.

Herne's power as an actor had become evident as early as his San Francisco days in the 1870s. His performance there as Rip Van Winkle was exceptional, causing David Belasco to comment:

> I have seen three *Rips*,—that of Jefferson, that of Robert McWade, and finally that of James A. Herne. This last was a wonderful characterization, with all the softness and pathos of the part. . . . Jefferson was never the Dutchman; he was the Yankee personating the Dutchman. But James A. Herne's *Rip* was the real thing.[17]

Herne advocated and practiced realistic acting even before it had taken hold in Europe through the work of André Antoine, Stanislavsky, and other directors of the realistic school. As a director, Herne insisted upon ensemble playing and refused to cater to stars. His own performances were always marked by restraint and attention to physical details. He had a limited voice, but his use of his hands for telling effect was widely noted by his appreciative critics. In Herne's company for *Sag Harbor* was an aspiring young performer named Lionel Barrymore, who wrote of his director: "Mr. Herne was one of the greatest actors that ever lived, a great man in his own right quite aside from acting, and he was a kind man."[18]

Herne wrote only two plays after *Shore Acres*, neither of which was very successful: *The Reverend Griffith Davenport* (Herald Square Theatre, January 31, 1899) and *Sag Harbor* (Republic Theatre, September 27, 1900), a reworking of *Hearts of Oak*. *Griffith Davenport* is a drama of the Civil War that can be evaluated today only secondhand, for only its fourth act survives. Nonetheless, Perry has called it "America's finest nineteenth century military drama."[19] It was the only one of several Civil War dramas to focus on the issue of slavery and deal honestly with the character of the black man. Herne's treatment of the black slaves in *Griffith Davenport* was realistic and far removed from the romanticized happy "nigger" types of Boucicault's *The Octoroon*. It is indeed unfortunate that the play has not survived intact; William Archer considered it the "cornerstone of a national drama."[20]

Much has been written of the influence of Henrik Ibsen's plays upon Herne's dramaturgy, but perhaps a more potent influence was that of Charles Dickens. Herne repeatedly expressed his admiration for Dickens's novels. He had played *Oliver Twist* in 1869 and written his own version of the work for staging in San Francisco in 1874. From Dickens, Herne learned the importance of detail in recreating nature through art;

a Boston critic in 1896 noted the influence of Dickens's character drawing upon the figures of *Shore Acres*.

Realistic characterization was surely the foundation of Herne's art as a dramatist. Of the convincing and compelling figures who populate his plays, Arthur Hobson Quinn remarked:

> They are not types: they are individuals. They remain in the memory—real people—for us to speculate upon their merits and defects, to wonder whether they really did the things their creator made them do, in short to become citizens of that world which is the product of close observation and powerful imagination.[21]

James A. Herne, the American Ibsen, died on June 2, 1901, of pleuropneumonia, at his Long Island home, Herne Oaks.

NOTES

1. Genesis

1. Paul Leicester Ford, "The Beginnings of American Dramatic Literature," *New England Magazine*, n.s. 9 (Feb., 1894), p. 675.
2. The single surviving copy of *Androboros* is housed in the Henry E. Huntington Library at San Marino, California. The play had what was probably its world premiere at the University of Southern California in November, 1979, directed by Peter Davis. Davis's research has revealed that the title-page date of 1714 is erroneous, although he has been unable to determine the actual date of publication.
3. *The Disappointment* was recently edited by David Mays and published in the American Revolution Bicentennial series of the University Presses of Florida (Gainesville, 1976).
4. Walter J. Meserve, *An Emerging Entertainment* (Bloomington, Indiana University Press, 1977), p. 49.
5. Arthur Hobson Quinn, *A History of the American Drama from the Beginning to the Civil War*, 2nd ed. (New York, Appleton-Century-Crofts, 1943), p. 30.
6. Quoted in Meserve, *Emerging Entertainment*, p. 69.
7. Quoted in Quinn, *History*, p. 34.
8. Ibid., p. 46.

2. America's First Comedy

1. Quoted in G. Thomas Tanselle, *Royall Tyler* (Cambridge, Mass., Harvard University Press, 1967), p. 5.
2. Ibid., p. 11.
3. All four plays may be found in Barrett H. Clark, gen. ed., *America's Lost Plays* (1941; reprint ed., Bloomington, Indiana University Press, 1963–65), vol. 15.

4. Dunlap's Contemporaries

1. Arthur Hobson Quinn, *A History of the American Drama from the Beginning to the Civil War*, 2nd ed. (New York, Appleton-Century-Crofts, 1943), p. 117.
2. Walter J. Meserve, *An Emerging Entertainment* (Bloomington, Indiana University Press, 1977), pp. 119–20.
3. Quoted in Richard Moody, ed., *Dramas from the American Theatre: 1762–1909* (Cleveland, World Publishing, 1966), p. 65.
4. Quoted in Richard Moody, *America Takes the Stage* (Bloomington, Indiana University Press, 1955), pp. 211–12.
5. Preface to *She Would Be a Soldier*.
6. Quoted in Montrose J. Moses, ed., *Representative Plays by American Dramatists* (New York, Benjamin Blom, 1964), vol. 1, p. 636.
7. Ibid., p. 568.
8. Robert Rogers's *Ponteach*, discussed in Chapter 1, is the first extant Indian play, but it was not acted.
9. Quoted in Meserve, *Emerging Entertainment*, p. 181.
10. Quinn, *History*, p. 140.
11. Ibid., pp. 140–41.
12. Ibid., p. 151.
13. Meserve, *Emerging Entertainment*, p. 184.

5. Enter the Actor-Dramatist

1. Quoted in Grace Overmyer, *America's First Hamlet* (Westport, Conn., Greenwood Press, reprinted 1975), p. 62.
2. Ibid., p. 83.
3. Ibid., p. 215.
4. Ibid., p. 263.
5. Ibid., p. 232.
6. Quoted in Eric Wollencott Barnes, *The Lady of Fashion* (New York, Charles Scribner's Sons, 1954), pp. 4–5.
7. Ibid., p. 47.
8. Ibid., p. 111.
9. Ibid., p. 193.
10. Ibid., p. 196.

6. The Romantic Movement

1. Arthur Hobson Quinn, *A History of the American Drama from the Beginning to the Civil War*, 2nd ed. (New York, Appleton-Century-Crofts, 1943), p. 236.
2. Four of these plays—*'Twas All for the Best* (1827), *The Cowled Lover* (1827), *Caridorf* (1827), and *News of the Night* (1828)—may be found in Barrett H. Clark, gen. ed., *America's Lost Plays* (1941; reprint ed., Bloomington, Indiana University Press, 1963–65), vol. 12.
3. Quoted in Quinn, *History*, p. 232.
4. Ibid., p. 236.
5. Quoted in Curtis Dahl, *Robert Montgomery Bird* (New York, Twayne, 1963), p. 59.
6. Quoted in Quinn, *History*, p. 243.
7. Ibid., p. 222.
8. Ibid., p. 337.
9. Ibid.
10. Quoted in Richard Moody, ed., *Dramas from the American Theatre: 1762–1909* (Cleveland, World Publishing, 1966), p. 425.

11. Quoted in Clark, *America's Lost Plays*, vol. 3, p. xii.
12. Quoted in Quinn, *History*, p. 347.
13. Ibid., p. 350.
14. Quoted in Moody, *Dramas*, p. 427.
15. Ibid., p. 428.
16. Ibid., p. 429.

7. *Dion Boucicault: Master of Melodrama*

1. Robert Hogan, *Dion Boucicault* (New York, Twayne, 1969), p. 47.
2. Quoted in Montrose J. Moses and John Mason Brown, eds., *The American Theatre as Seen by Its Critics: 1752–1934* (1934; reprint ed., New York, Cooper Square, 1967), p. 61.
3. Hogan, *Dion Boucicault*, p. 47.
4. Quoted in Townsend Walsh, *The Career of Dion Boucicault* (1915; reprint ed., New York, Benjamin Blom, 1967), p. 96.
5. Ibid., p. 94.
6. Hogan, *Dion Boucicault*, p. 65.
7. Walsh, *Career*, p. 126.
8. Ibid., p. 97.
9. Hogan, *Dion Boucicault*, p. 104.

8. *The Move toward Realism*

1. Arthur Hobson Quinn, *A History of the American Drama from the Civil War to the Present Day*, rev. ed., 2 vols. in 1 (New York, Appleton-Century-Crofts, 1936), vol. 1, p. 14.
2. Quoted in Marvin Felheim, *The Theater of Augustin Daly* (Cambridge, Mass., Harvard University Press, 1956), p. 287.
3. Ibid., p. 59.
4. From *Sixty Years in the Theatre* (1916); quoted in Montrose J. Moses and John Mason Brown, eds., *The*

American Theatre as Seen by Its Critics: 1752–1934 (1934; reprint ed., New York, Cooper Square, 1967), p. 114.

5. Felheim, *Theater*, p. 293.

6. Quoted in Moses and Brown, *American Theatre*, pp. 140–42.

7. Quoted in Richard Moody, ed., *Dramas from the American Theatre: 1762–1909* (Cleveland, World Publishing, 1966), p. 567.

8. Ibid., p. 571.

9. Realism Achieved

1. The texts of these four Belasco–De Mille plays may be found in Barrett H. Clark, gen. ed., *America's Lost Plays* (1941; reprint ed., Bloomington, Indiana University Press, 1963–65), vol. 17.

2. Arthur Hobson Quinn, *A History of the American Drama from the Civil War to the Present Day*, rev. ed., 2 vols. in 1 (New York, Appleton-Century-Crofts, 1936), vol. 1, p. 198.

3. David Belasco, *The Theatre Through Its Stage Door* (New York, Harper & Brothers, 1919), pp. 166–67.

4. It should be noted that Cecil B. De Mille was, to some extent, Belasco's collaborator in the writing of this play. De Mille's exact role can probably never be ascertained, but more than one commentator has accused Belasco of near plagiarism in claiming *Peter Grimm* as exclusively his own.

5. Quoted in Lise-Lone Marker, *David Belasco: Naturalism in the American Theatre* (Princeton, University Press, 1975), pp. 46–47.

6. Quoted in Craig Timberlake, *The Bishop of Broadway* (New York, Library Publishers, 1954), p. 220.

7. John Perry, *James A. Herne: The American Ibsen* (Chicago, Nelson-Hall, 1978). The writer is indebted to this excellent study of Herne for much of the information set forth in the present discussion of the dramatist and his works.

8. Ibid., p. 10.

9. Ibid., p. 66.

10. Ibid., p. 60.

11. Ibid., p. 132.

12. Quoted in Montrose J. Moses and John Mason Brown, eds., *The American Theatre as Seen by Its Critics: 1752–1934* (1934; reprint ed., New York, Cooper Square, 1967), p. 143.

13. Quoted in Richard Moody, ed., *Dramas from the American Theatre: 1762–1909* (Cleveland, World Publishing, 1966), p. 659.

14. Ibid., p. 666.

15. Perry, *Herne*, pp. 193–94.

16. Ibid., p. 239.

17. Ibid., pp. 28–29.

18. Ibid., p. 276.

19. Ibid., p. 8.

20. Ibid., p. 258.

21. Quinn, *History*, vol. 1, pp. 160–61.

BIBLIOGRAPHY

1. Sources for the Plays Discussed

Since early American plays are infrequently anthologized, they are somewhat difficult to locate. The following guide cites the most easily accessible sources for the texts of plays discussed in this volume. Plays are listed alphabetically by title, followed by the dramatist's surname and the letter codes for the anthologies in which the play may be found. Letter codes to the collections are as follows:

ALP   Clark, Barrett H., gen. ed. *America's Lost Plays.* 20 vols. 1941. Reprint (20 vols. in 10). Bloomington, Ind.: Indiana University Press, 1963–65. (Letter code is followed by volume no.)

BP   Gassner, John, ed. *Best Plays of the Early American Theatre.* New York: Crown Publishers, 1967.

AP   Halline, Allan Gates, ed. *American Plays.* New York: American Book Co., 1935.

LAC   *The Microbook Library of American Civilization.* Chicago: Library Resources, 1971. (Letter code is followed by Microcard no.)

DAT   Moody, Richard, ed. *Dramas from the American Theatre: 1762–1909.* Cleveland: World Publishing, 1966.

RAD   Moses, Montrose J., ed. *Representative American Dramas: National and Local.* Boston: Little, Brown & Co., 1925.

RPAD   Moses, Montrose J., ed. *Representative Plays by American Dramatists.* 3 vols. Reprinted. New York: Benjamin Blom, 1964. (Letter code is followed by volume no.)

RAP   Quinn, Arthur Hobson, ed. *Representative American Plays.* 7th ed. New York: Appleton-Century-Crofts, 1957.

Additionally, all of the plays discussed in this volume that were published in America prior to 1830 are included in the Readex Microprint series, "Three Centuries of English and American Plays," ed. Henry W. Wells, 1963.

THE PLAYS

Adulateur, The. Warren. LAC 40140
André. Dunlap. AP RAP RPAD I
Androboros. Hunter. LAC 40140
Battle of Bunker's Hill, The. Brackenridge. RPAD I
Broker of Bogota, The. Bird. RAP
Brutus. Payne. LAC 40054 RPAD II
Bunker-Hill. Burk. DAT
Candidates, The. Munford. DAT LAC 10068
Charles the Second. Payne–Irving. BP LAC 40054 RAP
Clari. Payne. Available only in eds. of 1823, 1832, 1835(?), & 1856
Colleen Bawn, The. Boucicault. In George Rowell, ed. *Nineteenth Century Plays.* 2nd ed. London: Oxford University Press, 1972
Contrast, The. Tyler. AP BP DAT LAC 12102 RAP RPAD I
Death of General Montgomery, The. Brackenridge. In Norman Philbrick, comp. *Trumpets Sounding . . .* New York: Benjamin Blom, 1972
Fall of British Tyranny, The. Leacock. LAC 40140 RPAD I

Fashion. Mowatt. AP BP DAT RAP RPAD II
Francesca da Rimini. Boker. AP DAT LAC
 13601-2 RAP RPAD III
Girl of the Golden West, The. Belasco. RAD Also
 in David Belasco. *Six Plays*. Boston: Little, Brown
 & Co., 1928
Gladiator, The. Bird. AP DAT
Glaucus. Boker. ALP III
Group, The. Warren. LAC 40054 RPAD I
Heart of Maryland, The. Belasco. ALP XVIII
Henrietta, The. Howard. AP
Horizon. Daly. AP
Indian Princess, The. Barker. RPAD I
London Assurance. Boucicault. In J. O. Bailey, ed.
 British Plays of the Nineteenth Century. New York:
 Odyssey Press, 1966.
Margaret Fleming. Herne. RAP
Marmion. Barker. Available only in eds. of 1812,
 1816, & 1826
Octoroon, The. Boucicault. BP LAC 40054 RAP
Patriots, The. Munford. LAC 10068
Ponteach. Rogers. LAC 14038 RPAD I
Poor of New York, The. Boucicault. LAC 40054
Prince of Parthia, The. Godfrey. LAC 15310 RAP
 RPAD I
Return of Peter Grimm, The. Belasco. RPAD III
 Also in Belasco, *Six Plays*
Richelieu. Payne–Irving. Available only in orig. eds.
 of 1826
Rip Van Winkle. Jefferson, Boucicault, et al. RAP
Shaughraun, The. Boucicault. In Michael Booth, ed.
 English Plays of the Nineteenth Century. Oxford:
 Clarendon Press, 1969
Shenandoah. Howard. DAT RAP RPAD III
She Would Be a Soldier. Noah. RPAD I
Shore Acres. Herne. DAT
Superstition. Barker. AP BP RAP
Trip to Niagara, A. Dunlap. DAT
Under the Gaslight. Daly. In Michael Booth, ed.
 Hiss the Villain. New York: Benjamin Blom, 1964

2. Secondary Sources

Barnes, Eric Wollencott. *The Lady of Fashion*. New York: Charles Scribner's Sons, 1954. (Biography of Anna Cora Mowatt Ritchie)

Belasco, David. *The Theatre Through Its Stage Door*. New York: Harper & Brothers, 1919.

Bost, James S. *Monarchs of the Mimic World*. Orono: University of Maine at Orono Press, 1977.

Canary, Robert H. *William Dunlap*. New York: Twayne Publishers, 1970.

Carson, Ada Lou, and Carson, Herbert L. *Royall Tyler*. Boston: Twayne Publishers, 1979.

Coad, Oral Sumner. *William Dunlap*. New York: Russell & Russell, 1962.

Dahl, Curtis. *Robert Montgomery Bird*. New York: Twayne Publishers, 1963.

Daly, Joseph Francis. *The Life of Augustin Daly*. New York: The Macmillan Co., 1917.

Fawkes, Richard. *Dion Boucicault*. London: Quartet Books, 1979.

Felheim, Marvin. *The Theater of Augustin Daly*. Cambridge, Mass.: Harvard University Press, 1956.

Hogan, Robert. *Dion Boucicault*. New York: Twayne Publishers, 1969.

Hornblow, Arthur. *A History of the Theatre in America*. 2 vols. Reprinted. New York: Benjamin Blom, 1965.

Kirk, Clara M., and Kirk, Rudolf. *William Dean Howells*. New York: Twayne Publishers, 1962.

Marker, Lise-Lone. *David Belasco: Naturalism in the American Theatre*. Princeton, N. J.: Princeton University Press, 1975.

Meserve, Walter J. *An Emerging Entertainment: The Drama of the American People to 1828*. Bloomington, Ind.: Indiana University Press, 1977.

Moody, Richard. *America Takes the Stage*. Bloomington, Ind.: Indiana University Press, 1955.

Moses, Montrose J., and Brown, John Mason, eds. *The American Theatre as Seen by Its Critics: 1752–1934.* 1934. Reprint. New York: Cooper Square Publishers, 1967.

Overmyer, Grace. *America's First Hamlet.* Reprint. Westport, Conn.: Greenwood Press, 1975. (Biography of John Howard Payne).

Perry, John. *James A. Herne: The American Ibsen.* Chicago: Nelson-Hall, 1978.

Quinn, Arthur Hobson. *A History of the American Drama from the Beginning to the Civil War.* 2nd ed. New York: Appleton-Century-Crofts, 1951.

————. *A History of the American Drama from the Civil War to the Present Day.* 2 vols. 1927. Rev. ed. (2 vols. in 1). New York: Appleton-Century-Crofts, 1936.

Tanselle, G. Thomas. *Royall Tyler.* Cambridge, Mass.: Harvard University Press, 1967.

Timberlake, Craig. *The Bishop of Broadway.* New York: Library Publishers, 1954. (Study of David Belasco).

Walsh, Townsend. *The Career of Dion Boucicault.* Reprint. New York: Benjamin Blom, 1967.

Wilson, Garff B. *Three Hundred Years of American Drama and Theatre.* Englewood Cliffs, N.J.: Prentice-Hall, 1973.

INDEX